SORROWS OF THE SOUL

DIPAN KUMAR DAS

SUDIP KUMAR DAS

To those who have weathered the storms of sorrow, whose resilience and courage inspire us to explore the depths of the human soul.

To all those who have felt the weight of sorrow in their hearts,

May this book offer solace, understanding, and hope

In navigating the depths of the soul's sorrows

And discovering the strength within to endure and grow.

Foreword

In the journey of life, sorrow is an inevitable companion that touches each of us in unique and profound ways. It is an emotion that transcends boundaries of culture, age, and circumstance, leaving its mark on the human experience. In "Sorrows of the Soul," the reader is invited into a thoughtful exploration of this complex emotion.

This book delves deep into the origins, manifestations, and impacts of sorrow, offering insights drawn from psychology, sociology, literature, and personal narratives. It seeks to unravel the mysteries of sorrow, challenging us to confront its discomforts while discovering its hidden potentials for growth and resilience.

Through meticulous research and heartfelt storytelling, the chapters unfold a tapestry of understanding—from the biological roots of sorrow to its cultural expressions, from the ways it shapes our identities to the healing paths we can embark upon. Each page invites reflection and empathy, encouraging readers to recognize their own sorrows and those of others with compassion.

As you embark on this exploration, may you find comfort in knowing that sorrow, though often painful, is also a catalyst for profound transformation. May this book illuminate the shadows of sorrow, revealing the resilience of the human spirit and the beauty of finding meaning amidst life's trials.

Preface

"Sorrows of the Soul" began as a personal quest to understand the intricate layers of sorrow—the emotion that touches every human heart in its own time and way. This book is not just an exploration of sorrow itself, but an invitation to delve into its depths with curiosity, compassion, and courage.

In these pages, you will encounter stories of individuals grappling with sorrow, scientific insights into its psychological and physiological dimensions, and cultural perspectives that shape our understanding of this universal emotion. Through literature, art, and personal narratives, we aim to paint a holistic picture of sorrow's impact on our lives and its potential for growth and healing.

My journey into the world of sorrow has been both enlightening and humbling. It has taught me that sorrow is not merely a burden to bear but a transformative force that can lead to resilience, empathy, and profound personal growth. By exploring sorrow with open hearts and minds, we can learn to navigate its challenges and discover its hidden gifts.

I hope that "Sorrows of the Soul" serves as a guide and companion for anyone seeking to understand their own sorrows or support others in their journey. May it offer insights, comfort, and inspiration as we navigate the complexities of the human experience together.

Prologue

In the quiet recesses of our hearts, there resides a chamber where sorrows dwell—a place where emotions run deep and memories linger. It is within this realm that the journey of "Sorrows of the Soul" begins, a journey that seeks to unravel the intricacies of an emotion as old as humanity itself.

Sorrow is not a mere fleeting sentiment but a profound experience that shapes our understanding of life, love, and loss. It transcends language and culture, touching the lives of individuals across time and space. In this prologue, we set forth on a quest to explore the multifaceted nature of sorrow, guided by stories that illuminate its essence and its impact on the human spirit.

Through the lens of psychology, philosophy, and personal narrative, we venture into the heart of sorrow, seeking to understand its origins and manifestations. We confront the paradoxes it presents: how sorrow can coexist with resilience, how it deepens our capacity for empathy, and how it fosters personal growth amidst adversity.

As we embark on this journey together, let us embrace the complexities of sorrow with empathy and insight. May this exploration not only illuminate the shadows of our hearts but also illuminate the path toward healing, understanding, and resilience.

Welcome to "Sorrows of the Soul."

CHAPTER ONE

Understanding Sorrow

Definition of sorrow and its various forms

Sorrow is a complex and deeply felt emotion typically associated with feelings of sadness, loss, grief, or regret. It often arises in response to events such as the death of a loved one, personal failures, or other significant losses. The intensity and expression of sorrow can vary widely among individuals and cultures. Here are various forms of sorrow:

Grief:

Definition: A deep and poignant distress caused by or as if by bereavement.

Examples: The death of a loved one, the end of a significant relationship.

Mourning:

Definition: The process of expressing or experiencing sorrow over a death or loss.

Examples: Rituals and ceremonies such as funerals, wearing black clothing, sharing memories of the deceased.

Melancholy:

Definition: A deep, pensive, and long-lasting sadness.

Examples: Feeling persistently down without a clear cause, reflecting on the past with a sense of sadness.

Heartache:

Definition: Emotional anguish or grief, typically resulting from a significant emotional loss or disappointment.

Examples: The end of a romantic relationship, unfulfilled dreams or desires.

Regret:

Definition: A feeling of sorrow or remorse for something that has happened or been done.

Examples: Wishing one had made different choices, feeling sorry for past actions or inactions.

Despair:

Definition: The complete loss or absence of hope.

Examples: Experiencing a situation where one sees no positive outcome, chronic or severe depression.

Remorse:

Definition: Deep regret or guilt for a wrong committed.

Examples: Feeling guilty for hurting someone, regretting a harmful action or decision.

Bereavement:

Definition: The period of mourning and grief following the death of a loved one.

Examples: Adjusting to life without the deceased, experiencing emotional pain and sorrow.

Woe:

Definition: Great sorrow or distress.

Examples: Facing a series of misfortunes, experiencing deep emotional suffering.

Desolation:

Definition: A state of complete emptiness or destruction; anguished misery or loneliness.

Examples: Feeling abandoned or utterly alone, experiencing profound loss or hopelessness.

Each form of sorrow has its unique characteristics and is often accompanied by specific behaviors, thoughts, and physical sensations. Understanding these distinctions can help in identifying and addressing one's own feelings or those of others.

Historical and cultural perspectives on sorrow

The experience and expression of sorrow have varied significantly across different historical periods and cultures. These perspectives often reflect broader societal values, religious beliefs, and philosophical outlooks. Here are some historical and cultural perspectives on sorrow:

Historical Perspectives

Ancient Greece:

Philosophical Views: Philosophers like Aristotle and Plato viewed sorrow (often referred to as "pathos") as a fundamental human emotion. Aristotle discussed it in the context of tragedy, suggesting that the experience of sorrow through art could lead to catharsis—a cleansing of emotions.

Literature: Homer's epics, such as "The Iliad," portray sorrow in the context of heroism and the human condition. Characters express profound grief and sorrow, which are seen as noble responses to loss and suffering.

Medieval Europe:

Religious Influence: Christianity profoundly shaped views on sorrow. The concept of "vale of tears" reflects the belief that life is a pilgrimage marked by suffering and sorrow, leading ultimately to salvation. Mourning and penance were seen as necessary for spiritual purification.

Rituals and Practices: Elaborate mourning rituals, including the wearing of black, public displays of grief, and memorial masses, were common.

Renaissance and Enlightenment:

Humanism: Renaissance humanism brought a shift towards understanding sorrow through the lens of individual experience and psychological depth. Literature and art explored personal grief and melancholy.

Philosophical Shifts: Enlightenment thinkers like Rousseau emphasized natural human emotions, including sorrow, as essential to the human experience.

Cultural Perspectives

Asian Cultures:

Buddhism: Sorrow is seen as one of the inevitable aspects of human existence, tied to the concept of dukkha (suffering). The path to enlightenment involves understanding and transcending sorrow through practices like meditation and mindfulness.

Confucianism: Emphasizes the importance of mourning and filial piety. Grief is considered a moral duty, especially in the context of honoring one's parents and ancestors.

African Cultures:

Community and Rituals: Many African cultures emphasize communal expressions of sorrow. Funerals and mourning rituals often involve extended family and community participation, music, dance, and storytelling.

Spiritual Beliefs: Sorrow and mourning are connected to a belief in the spiritual world and the continued existence of the deceased's spirit.

Indigenous Cultures:

Holistic Views: Indigenous cultures often have a holistic approach to sorrow, viewing it as part of the natural cycle of life and death. Rituals and ceremonies help individuals and communities process grief and maintain a connection with ancestors.

Storytelling and Tradition: Oral traditions and storytelling play a crucial role in expressing and coping with sorrow, passing down wisdom and maintaining cultural continuity.

Western Contemporary Cultures:

Psychological Understanding: Modern psychology has contributed to understanding sorrow as a complex emotional state that can be addressed through therapy, support groups, and medication.

Cultural Shifts: There has been a shift towards more private expressions of sorrow, with an emphasis on personal grief management rather than public displays of mourning.

Comparative Summary

Religious vs. Secular: Historically, religious perspectives often framed sorrow as a necessary part of spiritual growth or divine plan, while modern secular views focus more on psychological and emotional well-being.

Collective vs. Individual: Many traditional cultures emphasize collective mourning and community support, whereas contemporary Western societies often focus on individual experiences and private grief.

Rituals and Practices: Across cultures and eras, rituals have been central to processing sorrow, though the form and significance of these rituals vary widely.

Understanding these perspectives can provide insight into how different societies cope with and give meaning to sorrow, reflecting broader cultural values and worldviews.

Differentiating sorrow from other emotions like sadness and grief

Sorrow, sadness, and grief are all interconnected emotions, but they have distinct characteristics and contexts in which they are typically experienced:

Sorrow

Definition: Sorrow is a deep and profound emotional response to loss, disappointment, or suffering. It often involves a sense of regret, longing, or despair.

Characteristics:

Intense Emotional Depth: Sorrow is often characterized by a deep, poignant emotional experience that can feel overwhelming.

Longing or Regret: It may involve feelings of yearning for what has been lost or regret over past actions or decisions.

Reflective and Pensive: Sorrow often leads to introspection and contemplation about the nature of loss and its impact.

Sadness

Definition: Sadness is a general emotional state characterized by feelings of unhappiness, melancholy, or low spirits. It can be triggered by various circumstances, not just loss.

Characteristics:

Temporary State: Sadness tends to be more transient and can fluctuate based on circumstances or events.

Milder Intensity: While sadness can be intense, it is typically not as deep or overwhelming as sorrow.

Cause-specific: Sadness can arise from a wide range of situations, such as disappointment, loneliness, or frustration, not just from loss.

Grief

Definition: Grief is a multifaceted response to loss, particularly the loss of someone or something to which a bond was formed. It involves emotional, psychological, and physical reactions.

Characteristics:

Complex Emotional Process: Grief unfolds over time and involves a range of emotions, including sorrow, sadness, anger, and even guilt.

Manifests in Stages: Grief often progresses through stages, such as denial, anger, bargaining, depression, and acceptance, as outlined in Kübler-Ross's model.

Contextual: Grief is specifically tied to the experience of loss and the need to adjust to life without the person or thing that has been lost.

Key Differences

Depth and Duration: Sorrow tends to be deeper and more enduring than sadness, which is often more fleeting. Grief, while encompassing sorrow, is a broader process involving multiple emotional states.

Context: Sorrow is particularly tied to a sense of regret or longing, while sadness can stem from various causes, and grief specifically pertains to loss and its aftermath.

Processing: Grief involves a structured emotional and psychological process of coming to terms with loss, whereas sorrow and sadness may not always lead to such a structured journey.

In summary, while sorrow, sadness, and grief are related emotions that often coexist, they differ in terms of depth, duration, context, and the emotional processes involved. Understanding these distinctions can help individuals and professionals better navigate and support those experiencing these complex emotions.

The role of sorrow in human experience and development

Sorrow plays a significant role in the human experience and development, influencing individuals in profound ways across various dimensions—emotional, psychological, social, and even spiritual. Here are key aspects of the role of sorrow:

Emotional Depth and Understanding

Facilitates Emotional Growth: Sorrow allows individuals to explore and understand the depth of their emotional capacity. It enables them to confront and process complex feelings such as regret, longing, and sadness, which are essential for emotional maturity.

Promotes Empathy and Compassion: Experiencing sorrow can increase empathy towards others who are suffering or grieving. It fosters a deeper understanding of human vulnerability and strengthens interpersonal connections through shared experiences of loss.

Psychological Development

Resilience and Coping Mechanisms: Coping with sorrow challenges individuals to develop resilience and adaptive coping strategies. Overcoming sorrow involves navigating through grief stages (denial, anger, bargaining, depression, acceptance), fostering personal growth and psychological strength.

Self-Reflection and Personal Growth: Sorrow prompts individuals to reflect on their beliefs, values, and life choices. This introspection can lead to personal growth, as it encourages them to reassess priorities, develop resilience, and cultivate a deeper sense of meaning and purpose in life.

Social and Cultural Significance

Community and Support Systems: Sorrow often brings communities together, fostering support networks and rituals that help individuals navigate grief collectively. Cultural practices surrounding sorrow, such as mourning rituals and ceremonies, provide frameworks for expressing and processing grief within societal norms.

Identity and Meaning-Making: Sorrow can shape individual identity and cultural identity. It influences how individuals perceive themselves in relation to others and their understanding of life's challenges and uncertainties. Cultural and religious beliefs about sorrow contribute to shaping individual perspectives on loss and grief.

Spiritual and Existential Dimensions

Exploration of Existential Questions: Sorrow often prompts individuals to contemplate existential questions about life, death, and the nature of human existence. This exploration can lead to a deeper spiritual awareness and a search for meaning beyond immediate suffering.

Transformation and Transcendence: Through sorrow, individuals may undergo transformative experiences that transcend personal suffering. It can inspire personal growth, resilience, and a renewed sense of purpose, leading to spiritual growth and a deeper connection with oneself and others.

Conclusion

In summary, sorrow is a profound and multifaceted emotion that plays a crucial role in human development and experience. It challenges individuals to confront and navigate complex emotions, fosters empathy and resilience, shapes personal and cultural identities, and prompts existential reflection and spiritual growth. While inherently painful, sorrow ultimately contributes to emotional maturity, personal development, and the capacity for compassion and understanding in individuals and communities alike.

Psychological and physiological effects of sorrow

Sorrow, being a deeply emotional and often prolonged state, can have significant psychological and physiological effects on individuals. These effects can manifest across various dimensions of human experience:

Psychological Effects

Emotional Distress: Sorrow is characterized by intense emotional pain, sadness, and grief. It can lead to feelings of despair, hopelessness, and a sense of emptiness or numbness.

Cognitive Impact: Sorrow can affect cognitive functions such as concentration, memory, and decision-making. Individuals may find it challenging to focus on tasks or make clear judgments while experiencing intense sorrow.

Mood Disorders: Prolonged sorrow can contribute to the development or exacerbation of mood disorders such as depression or anxiety. It may also increase vulnerability to conditions like post-traumatic stress disorder (PTSD), especially if the sorrow is related to a traumatic event.

Self-Esteem and Identity: Sorrow can impact self-esteem and self-perception. Individuals may question their beliefs, values, or their ability to cope with challenges, leading to a sense of diminished self-worth or identity crisis.

Social Withdrawal: People experiencing sorrow may withdraw from social interactions or activities they once enjoyed. This withdrawal can lead to feelings of isolation, loneliness, and difficulty in seeking or accepting support from others.

Physiological Effects

Stress Response: Sorrow triggers the body's stress response, leading to increased production of stress hormones such as cortisol. Prolonged activation of the stress response can have negative effects on physical health, including cardiovascular function, immune response, and metabolism.

Sleep Disturbances: Many individuals experiencing sorrow may struggle with sleep disturbances such as insomnia or disrupted sleep patterns. This can further exacerbate feelings of fatigue, irritability, and difficulty concentrating.

Physical Health Impact: Chronic sorrow can contribute to physical health issues such as headaches, digestive problems, muscle tension, and overall weakened immune function. The body's ability to heal and recover from illness may also be compromised.

Pain Perception: Research suggests that emotional pain, including sorrow, can alter the perception of physical pain. Individuals experiencing sorrow may have a lower pain threshold or heightened sensitivity to physical discomfort.

Appetite and Weight Changes: Sorrow can affect appetite and eating behaviors, leading to either decreased or increased food intake. Changes in appetite can contribute to weight fluctuations and nutritional imbalances, impacting overall health.

Coping Strategies and Interventions

Addressing the psychological and physiological effects of sorrow often requires a comprehensive approach that combines emotional support, therapeutic interventions, and self-care strategies:

Therapeutic Support: Counseling or psychotherapy can help individuals explore and process their feelings of sorrow in a supportive environment. Cognitive-behavioral techniques and mindfulness practices may be particularly beneficial.

Social Support: Building and maintaining strong social connections can provide emotional support and reduce feelings of isolation. Support groups or peer networks specifically for grief and loss can offer validation and understanding.

Physical Health Practices: Engaging in regular physical activity, maintaining a balanced diet, and prioritizing adequate sleep can support overall well-being and help mitigate some of the physiological effects of sorrow.

Mind-Body Techniques: Practices such as yoga, meditation, deep breathing exercises, and progressive muscle relaxation can help reduce stress, promote relaxation, and improve emotional resilience.

Medication: In some cases, medication prescribed by a healthcare professional may be necessary to manage symptoms of depression, anxiety, or sleep disturbances associated with prolonged sorrow.

By addressing both the psychological and physiological aspects of sorrow through appropriate interventions and support systems, individuals can work towards healing, resilience, and a renewed sense of emotional well-being over time.

CHAPTER TWO

The Origins of Sorrow

Biological and evolutionary basis of sorrow

Sorrow, like other emotions, has deep biological and evolutionary roots. Emotions are complex responses that involve physiological, psychological, and behavioral components. Here's an overview of the biological and evolutionary basis of sorrow:

Biological Basis of Sorrow

Brain Regions Involved:

Amygdala: The amygdala plays a crucial role in processing emotions, including sorrow. It helps in the evaluation of emotional stimuli and the generation of appropriate emotional responses.

Prefrontal Cortex: This region is involved in the regulation and modulation of emotions. It helps in interpreting and responding to emotional experiences, including those that cause sorrow.

Hippocampus: This part of the brain is associated with memory and can link memories with emotions. Experiences of sorrow are often connected to memories of loss or trauma.

Insula: This area is involved in emotional awareness and empathy, which are critical in experiencing sorrow, especially in response to others' suffering.

Neurotransmitters:

Serotonin: Often associated with mood regulation, low levels of serotonin are linked to depression and feelings of sadness.

Dopamine: Involved in reward and pleasure pathways, decreased dopamine activity can contribute to feelings of sorrow.

Norepinephrine: This neurotransmitter is involved in stress responses and can influence mood and emotional responses.

Hormones:

Cortisol: Known as the stress hormone, elevated levels of cortisol can result from chronic stress and are often associated with prolonged feelings of sadness and sorrow.

Oxytocin: Often called the "love hormone," oxytocin is involved in social bonding and can influence feelings of empathy and sorrow, especially in social contexts.

Evolutionary Basis of Sorrow

Social Bonds and Group Cohesion:

Strengthening Social Bonds: Sorrow, especially in the context of loss or grief, can strengthen social bonds within a group. When individuals express sorrow, it can elicit support and empathy from others, reinforcing group cohesion.

Promoting Altruism: Sorrow and empathy are closely linked. Experiencing sorrow in response to another's suffering can promote altruistic behavior, which is beneficial for group survival.

Learning and Avoidance:

Adaptive Responses to Loss: Sorrow can be a powerful motivator for learning. Negative experiences and the sorrow associated with them can lead to behaviors that avoid future losses or harmful situations.

Memory Consolidation: Emotional experiences, including sorrow, enhance memory consolidation. This means that sorrowful experiences can be more vividly remembered, which can help individuals learn from past mistakes.

Signaling Mechanism:

Communication of Need: Expressions of sorrow, such as crying or withdrawal, can signal to others that an individual needs support or help. This can prompt assistance from others, enhancing the individual's chances of recovery and survival.

Social Signals: Visible signs of sorrow can communicate the seriousness of a situation to others, prompting a coordinated group response to threats or losses.

Conclusion

Sorrow is a complex emotion with a deep biological basis involving specific brain regions, neurotransmitters, and hormones. Evolutionarily, sorrow plays a crucial role in social bonding, learning, and communication. It helps individuals and groups navigate and adapt to challenges, ultimately enhancing survival and cohesion. Understanding the biological and evolutionary underpinnings of sorrow provides insight into its significance in human behavior and social structures.

Genetic and hereditary influences

Genetic and hereditary influences play significant roles in shaping how individuals experience and respond to emotions like sorrow. Here's an exploration of these influences:

Genetic Influences

Gene Variants and Risk Factors:

Serotonin Transporter Gene (SLC6A4): Variants of this gene have been linked to differences in serotonin reuptake, affecting mood regulation. Certain variants may predispose individuals to higher susceptibility to sadness and sorrow.

BDNF (Brain-Derived Neurotrophic Factor) Gene: BDNF is involved in neuronal growth and survival. Variants in this gene have been associated with mood disorders, including depression, which can manifest with profound feelings of sorrow.

COMT (Catechol-O-Methyltransferase) Gene: This gene regulates dopamine levels in the brain. Variants can influence how effectively dopamine is broken down, impacting emotional responses and vulnerability to sadness.

MAOA (Monoamine Oxidase A) Gene: Variants of this gene affect the breakdown of neurotransmitters like serotonin and dopamine, influencing emotional regulation and responses to stress and sorrow.

Heritability of Emotional Traits:

Family Studies: Research indicates that emotional traits, including susceptibility to sadness and sorrow, can run in families. This suggests a genetic component in how individuals perceive and react to emotional stimuli.

Twin Studies: Studies on identical and fraternal twins have shown that genetic factors contribute significantly to the variability in emotional responses, including sorrow.

Hereditary Influences

Family Dynamics and Social Learning:

Modeling of Emotional Responses: Children often learn emotional responses, including expressions of sorrow, through observation and interaction with family members. This can shape how they express and cope with sorrowful experiences later in life.

Cultural and Environmental Factors: While genetic predispositions play a role, environmental factors within the family, such as parenting style and family dynamics, also influence how sorrow is expressed and managed.

Epigenetic Factors:

Environmental Influences: Epigenetic mechanisms can modify gene expression without altering the underlying DNA sequence. Environmental factors such as stress, nutrition, and early life experiences can influence epigenetic changes that affect emotional regulation and responses to sorrow.

Interaction of Genetics and Environment

Gene-Environment Interactions: The expression of genetic predispositions to sorrow can be influenced by environmental factors. For example, individuals with genetic variants associated with increased susceptibility to sadness may exhibit varying levels of sorrow depending on their life experiences and stress levels.

Resilience and Adaptation: Genetic predispositions do not determine an individual's destiny. Resilience factors, including supportive relationships, coping strategies, and access to mental health resources, can mitigate the impact of genetic predispositions and help individuals manage sorrow effectively.

Conclusion

Genetic and hereditary influences on sorrow involve complex interactions between specific gene variants, familial dynamics, and broader environmental factors. While genetic predispositions can contribute to individual differences in emotional responses, the expression of sorrow is also shaped by social learning, cultural norms, and personal experiences. Understanding these influences can inform approaches to supporting individuals experiencing sorrow and developing personalized strategies for emotional well-being.

The impact of early childhood experiences and trauma

Early childhood experiences and trauma can have profound and lasting impacts on emotional development, including how individuals experience and cope with sorrow. Here are some key aspects of their impact:

Psychological and Emotional Development

Attachment Patterns:

Secure vs. Insecure Attachment: Early experiences of consistent nurturing and responsive caregiving promote secure attachment. Securely attached children tend to develop trust in relationships and have healthier emotional regulation, which can help them cope better with sorrow later in life.

Insecure Attachment: Children who experience inconsistent or neglectful caregiving may develop insecure attachment styles (e.g., anxious-ambivalent or avoidant). These attachment styles can lead to difficulties in regulating emotions, including sorrow, and may contribute to challenges in seeking comfort from others.

Emotional Regulation:

Developmental Milestones: Early childhood is a critical period for learning emotional regulation skills. Trauma or adverse experiences during this time can disrupt the development of effective coping strategies.

Impact on Stress Response: Early trauma can sensitize the stress response system, leading to heightened emotional reactivity and difficulties in managing emotions such as sorrow.

Cognitive and Behavioral Responses

Cognitive Schema:

Core Beliefs and Interpretations: Early experiences, especially those involving trauma, can shape cognitive schemas—core beliefs about oneself, others, and the world. Negative schemas can predispose individuals to interpret experiences in ways that exacerbate feelings of sorrow and hopelessness.

Cognitive Distortions: Trauma can contribute to the development of cognitive distortions (e.g., overgeneralization, personalization), which influence how individuals perceive and respond to emotional stimuli.

Behavioral Patterns:

Coping Mechanisms: Early experiences of trauma can impact the development of coping mechanisms. Individuals may develop maladaptive coping strategies (e.g., avoidance, substance use) to manage overwhelming feelings of sorrow.

Social Functioning: Trauma can affect social skills and interpersonal relationships, which are crucial for seeking support and comfort during times of sorrow.

Long-term Impact on Mental Health

Risk of Mental Health Disorders:

Increased Vulnerability: Early childhood trauma is associated with a higher risk of developing mental health disorders such as depression, anxiety disorders, and post-traumatic stress disorder (PTSD). These conditions can significantly amplify feelings of sorrow and make it more challenging to cope.

Complex Trauma and Cumulative Adversity:

Complex Trauma: Experiencing multiple or prolonged traumatic events (e.g., abuse, neglect, household dysfunction) can have cumulative effects on emotional and psychological development.

Adverse Childhood Experiences (ACEs): ACEs have been linked to a range of negative outcomes in adulthood, including poorer physical and mental health, substance abuse, and difficulties in relationships—all of which can contribute to heightened experiences of sorrow.

Resilience and Healing

Protective Factors:

Supportive Relationships: Positive relationships with caregivers, peers, and supportive adults can buffer the impact of early childhood trauma and promote resilience.

Therapeutic Interventions: Early intervention through trauma-informed therapy can help individuals process their experiences, develop healthier coping strategies, and heal emotional wounds associated with sorrow.

Trauma-Informed Care:

Understanding and Support: Creating environments that are sensitive to trauma history can foster healing and recovery. This approach emphasizes safety, trustworthiness, choice, collaboration, and empowerment.

Conclusion

Early childhood experiences and trauma profoundly shape emotional development, cognitive processing, and behavioral responses, influencing how individuals experience and cope with sorrow throughout their lives. Understanding these impacts can guide interventions and support systems aimed at promoting resilience, healing, and emotional well-being in individuals who have experienced early adversity.

Social and environmental factors contributing to sorrow

Sorrow, like other complex emotions, is influenced by a variety of social and environmental factors. These factors can significantly shape how individuals experience, express, and cope with sorrow. Here's an exploration of some key social and environmental contributors:

Social Factors

Loss and Grief:

Death of Loved Ones: Bereavement and grief following the loss of a loved one can evoke profound sorrow. The impact can vary depending on the relationship with the deceased and the circumstances of the loss.

Relationship Breakdowns: Divorce, separation, or the end of significant relationships can lead to feelings of sorrow and grief, especially if there was emotional investment or attachment involved.

Social Support:

Presence of Supportive Relationships: Having close relationships with family, friends, or community members who offer emotional support and empathy can mitigate the intensity and duration of sorrow.

Isolation and Loneliness: Lack of social support or feelings of loneliness can exacerbate feelings of sorrow, as individuals may struggle to find comfort or distraction from their emotions.

Cultural Norms and Beliefs:

Attitudes Towards Loss and Sorrow: Cultural beliefs and practices around grief and sorrow can influence how individuals perceive and express their emotions. Cultural norms may dictate mourning rituals, expectations for emotional expression, and support systems available.

Social Comparisons and Expectations:

Social Media and Comparisons: Exposure to idealized portrayals of happiness and success on social media can intensify feelings of sorrow, leading to comparisons and feelings of inadequacy.

Social Pressure: Expectations from society or peers regarding success, achievements, or milestones can contribute to feelings of sorrow if individuals perceive themselves as falling short or facing setbacks.

Environmental Factors

Life Events and Transitions:

Major Life Changes: Significant life events such as job loss, relocation, illness, or financial instability can trigger feelings of sorrow due to uncertainty, loss of routine, or dashed expectations.

Natural Disasters or Traumatic Events: Experiencing or witnessing natural disasters, accidents, or other traumatic events can lead to sorrow, grief, and emotional distress.

Socioeconomic Conditions:

Poverty and Economic Hardship: Living in poverty or facing economic instability can contribute to chronic stress, which may manifest as feelings of sorrow and hopelessness.

Access to Resources: Limited access to healthcare, education, employment opportunities, or supportive services can exacerbate feelings of sorrow, especially if individuals feel trapped in difficult circumstances.

Community and Social Dynamics:

Violence and Crime: Living in environments characterized by violence, crime, or social unrest can contribute to feelings of sorrow, fear, and trauma.

Social Inequality and Discrimination: Experiencing discrimination or marginalization based on race, ethnicity, gender, sexual orientation, or other factors can lead to profound feelings of sorrow and injustice.

Coping Mechanisms and Resilience

Personal Coping Strategies:

Healthy Coping Mechanisms: Engaging in activities such as exercise, hobbies, mindfulness, or creative outlets can help individuals manage and process feelings of sorrow.

Seeking Professional Help: Accessing therapy or counseling can provide individuals with tools to navigate sorrow and grief in a supportive and constructive manner.

Community and Institutional Support:

Support Groups and Networks: Participating in support groups or community organizations focused on grief and loss can provide validation, understanding, and shared experiences.

Workplace and Organizational Support: Employers and organizations that offer compassionate leave policies, employee assistance programs, or mental health resources can support individuals experiencing sorrow due to personal or professional challenges.

Conclusion

Sorrow is influenced by a complex interplay of social and environmental factors, reflecting the interconnected nature of human experiences. Understanding these contributors can inform supportive interventions and strategies aimed at promoting emotional well-being, resilience, and healing in individuals and communities facing sorrowful circumstances.

Personal narratives and case studies

Personal narratives and case studies provide rich insights into the diverse ways individuals experience and cope with sorrow. They offer a nuanced understanding of how social, environmental, and psychological factors intersect to shape emotional responses. Here are some illustrative examples and insights that personal narratives and case studies can provide:

Personal Narratives

Bereavement and Loss:

Example: A personal narrative might recount the profound sorrow experienced after the sudden death of a close family member. It could detail the stages of grief, from shock and disbelief to profound sadness and eventual acceptance.

Insight: Such narratives illuminate the unique ways individuals process loss and the importance of social support in navigating grief.

Traumatic Experiences:

Example: A narrative might describe the lingering sorrow and emotional scars following a traumatic event such as a car accident or natural disaster. It could explore how flashbacks and triggers evoke intense sorrow and anxiety.

Insight: These narratives highlight the long-term impact of trauma on emotional well-being and the challenges individuals face in rebuilding their lives.

Chronic Sorrow:

Example: A narrative from a parent of a child with a chronic illness might discuss the ongoing sorrow and grief associated with the child's health challenges. It could delve into the emotional rollercoaster of hope and despair in managing the condition.

Insight: Such narratives shed light on the complex emotions experienced by caregivers and their strategies for coping and finding resilience amidst ongoing challenges.

Case Studies

Cultural Perspectives on Grief:

Example: A case study might explore cultural variations in grieving practices and beliefs. It could compare how different cultural norms influence the expression and management of sorrow following loss.

Insight: Case studies provide a broader understanding of how cultural context shapes emotional responses and support systems for grieving individuals.

Impact of Social Support:

Example: A case study could examine the role of social support networks in mitigating sorrow. It might focus on how support from family, friends, or community organizations helps individuals cope with adversity and find meaning in their experiences.

Insight: These studies demonstrate the importance of social connections in promoting resilience and emotional well-being during times of sorrow.

Trauma and Recovery:

Example: A case study might document an individual's journey from trauma to recovery. It could detail therapeutic interventions, coping strategies, and milestones in healing from profound sorrow and post-traumatic stress.

Insight: Case studies provide evidence-based insights into effective treatment approaches and the factors that facilitate or hinder emotional recovery.

Insights and Contributions

Holistic Understanding: Personal narratives and case studies offer a holistic view of sorrow, encompassing individual experiences, cultural contexts, and the interplay of personal and social factors.

Informing Interventions: They inform therapeutic approaches, community support initiatives, and policy development aimed at addressing the needs of individuals experiencing sorrow and grief.

Empathy and Connection: By sharing personal stories, individuals and researchers foster empathy and understanding, reducing stigma and promoting compassionate responses to sorrowful experiences.

Conclusion

Personal narratives and case studies are invaluable sources of insight into the multifaceted nature of sorrow. They amplify individual voices, illuminate diverse experiences, and provide a deeper understanding of the factors that contribute to emotional responses and resilience in the face of sorrowful circumstances. Integrating these narratives into research and practice can enhance support systems and interventions tailored to meet the complex needs of individuals navigating sorrow.

CHAPTER THREE

Sorrow in Different Life Stages

Childhood and adolescent sorrow: causes and coping mechanisms

Childhood and adolescent sorrow, like sorrow experienced at any age, can stem from various causes and requires age-appropriate coping mechanisms to help young individuals navigate their emotions effectively. Here's an exploration of causes and coping mechanisms for childhood and adolescent sorrow:

Causes of Childhood and Adolescent Sorrow

Loss and Bereavement:

Death of a Loved One: Losing a family member, friend, or pet can be a significant source of sorrow for children and adolescents, especially if they have formed strong attachments.

Parental Divorce or Separation: Family disruptions such as divorce or separation can lead to feelings of sadness, confusion, and grief among children and teens.

Loss of Relationships: Ending friendships, moving to a new location, or experiencing rejection can also trigger feelings of sorrow and loneliness.

Trauma and Adversity:

Abuse or Neglect: Children and adolescents who have experienced physical, emotional, or sexual abuse, or neglect may carry deep sorrow and emotional pain.

Witnessing Violence or Accidents: Exposure to violence, accidents, or natural disasters can lead to feelings of fear, grief, and sorrow.

Chronic Illness or Disability:

Personal or Family Member's Illness: Coping with a chronic illness, either their own or that of a family member, can evoke sorrow and distress in children and adolescents.

Disability: Adjusting to a physical or developmental disability, either their own or a sibling's, can lead to feelings of sorrow and grief over perceived limitations or changes in family dynamics.

Academic or Social Challenges:

Academic Struggles: Difficulty in school, such as poor grades, bullying, or feeling academically inadequate, can lead to feelings of sadness and sorrow.

Social Rejection or Isolation: Being excluded from peer groups, experiencing bullying, or feeling socially isolated can contribute to feelings of loneliness and sorrow.

Coping Mechanisms for Childhood and Adolescent Sorrow

Emotional Expression and Communication:

Encouraging Open Dialogue: Creating a supportive environment where children and adolescents feel safe expressing their feelings of sorrow without judgment.

Art and Play Therapy: Engaging in creative activities such as drawing, painting, or storytelling can help younger children express and process their emotions.

Supportive Relationships:

Family Support: Providing unconditional love, understanding, and reassurance from caregivers and family members.

Peer Support: Encouraging healthy friendships and social connections can provide a sense of belonging and emotional support.

Educational Support and Structure:

School-based Counseling: Access to counselors or psychologists within the school setting who can provide emotional support and coping strategies.

Routine and Stability: Establishing predictable routines and structure can provide a sense of security and stability during times of sorrow.

Cognitive and Behavioral Strategies:

Cognitive Restructuring: Helping children and adolescents challenge negative thoughts and replace them with more positive and adaptive thinking patterns.

Relaxation Techniques: Teaching relaxation exercises, deep breathing, or mindfulness practices can help reduce stress and promote emotional well-being.

Physical Health and Well-being:

Healthy Lifestyle Choices: Encouraging regular physical activity, nutritious eating habits, and adequate sleep can support overall emotional resilience.

Limiting Stressors: Minimizing exposure to additional stressors or triggers that can exacerbate feelings of sorrow.

Professional Intervention:

Therapeutic Support: Seeking professional help from therapists or counselors specializing in child and adolescent psychology, especially in cases of prolonged or intense sorrow.

Medication: In severe cases or when symptoms of depression or anxiety are present, medication prescribed by a healthcare provider may be considered.

Conclusion

Childhood and adolescent sorrow can arise from a variety of causes, each requiring tailored coping strategies that take into account the developmental stage and unique needs of young individuals. By providing supportive environments, fostering healthy relationships, promoting emotional expression, and teaching effective coping skills, caregivers and educators can help children and adolescents navigate sorrow and build resilience for future challenges.

Sorrow in adulthood: career, relationships, and personal loss

Sorrow in adulthood can manifest in various dimensions of life, including career setbacks, challenges in relationships, and personal losses. Here's an exploration of how sorrow can affect adults in these areas and some coping mechanisms:

Career-related Sorrow

Job Loss or Career Setbacks:

Losing a job or experiencing setbacks in one's career can evoke feelings of sorrow, especially if it's unexpected or leads to financial insecurity.

Coping Mechanisms:

Seeking Support: Talking to friends, family, or career counselors for emotional support and practical advice.

Skill Development: Investing time in upgrading skills or exploring new career opportunities can provide a sense of direction and hope.

Maintaining Routine: Establishing a daily routine can help maintain a sense of stability and purpose during a career transition.

Unfulfilled Career Expectations:

Feeling dissatisfied or unfulfilled in one's career path can lead to sorrow over unrealized aspirations.

Coping Mechanisms:

Reevaluating Goals: Reflecting on personal values and long-term career aspirations to align with current circumstances.

Seeking Mentoring: Finding mentors or career coaches who can provide guidance and perspective on career decisions.

Exploring Alternatives: Considering alternative career paths or hobbies that can bring fulfillment outside of work.

Relationship-related Sorrow

Breakups or Divorce:

Ending a significant relationship can result in profound sorrow, grief, and feelings of loss.

Coping Mechanisms:

Processing Emotions: Allowing oneself to grieve the end of the relationship and seeking support from friends, family, or therapy.

Self-care: Engaging in activities that promote self-care and self-compassion, such as exercise, hobbies, or relaxation techniques.

Building Support Networks: Cultivating new friendships and social connections to combat feelings of loneliness.

Conflict or Estrangement:

Strained relationships with family members, friends, or colleagues can lead to feelings of sorrow and distress.

Coping Mechanisms:

Communication: Engaging in open and honest communication to address conflicts and repair relationships where possible.

Setting Boundaries: Establishing healthy boundaries to protect emotional well-being and minimize stress.

Seeking Mediation: In cases of significant conflict, seeking professional mediation or counseling to facilitate resolution.

Personal Loss-related Sorrow

Death of a Loved One:

Losing a family member, close friend, or pet can result in intense grief and sorrow.

Coping Mechanisms:

Grieving Process: Allowing oneself to mourn and process the loss in one's own time and way.

Seeking Support: Connecting with support groups, bereavement counseling, or spiritual communities for comfort and understanding.

Memorializing: Finding ways to honor and remember the loved one through rituals, traditions, or acts of tribute.

Health Issues or Chronic Illness:

Dealing with personal health challenges or chronic illness can lead to sorrow over changes in lifestyle, independence, or future expectations.

Coping Mechanisms:

Medical Support: Seeking medical treatment, advice, and support from healthcare professionals.

Adaptive Coping Strategies: Developing coping strategies to manage symptoms, maintain quality of life, and foster resilience.

Emotional Support: Engaging with support groups, therapy, or online communities for emotional support and shared experiences.

General Coping Mechanisms for Adult Sorrow

Self-care Practices: Prioritizing self-care through activities such as exercise, relaxation techniques, mindfulness, and adequate sleep.

Seeking Professional Help: Consulting with therapists, counselors, or support groups to process emotions and develop coping strategies.

Social Support: Building and maintaining strong social connections with friends, family, or support groups to alleviate feelings of isolation and loneliness.

Mindfulness and Acceptance: Practicing mindfulness techniques to stay present and accept difficult emotions without judgment.

Finding Meaning and Purpose: Engaging in activities or hobbies that bring joy, fulfillment, and a sense of purpose despite sorrowful circumstances.

By acknowledging and addressing sorrow in adulthood through these coping mechanisms, individuals can navigate challenges more effectively, promote emotional resilience, and cultivate a sense of hope for the future.

The sorrow of aging: facing mortality and loss of independence

The sorrow of aging encompasses a range of emotional and psychological challenges that individuals may face as they confront mortality, physical decline, and loss of independence. Here's an exploration of these aspects and strategies for coping:

Facing Mortality

Existential Reflection:

Awareness of Limited Time: As individuals age, they become increasingly aware of their mortality and the finite nature of life. This can lead to contemplation about the meaning and purpose of their existence.

Coping Mechanisms:

Finding Meaning: Engaging in activities that provide a sense of fulfillment and purpose, such as hobbies, volunteer work, or spending time with loved ones.

Spiritual Practices: Turning to spiritual beliefs or practices that offer comfort, guidance, and a sense of continuity beyond physical existence.

Grief and Loss:

Loss of Peers and Loved Ones: Aging often involves experiencing the deaths of friends, family members, and peers, which can lead to profound grief and sorrow.

Coping Mechanisms:

Grieving Process: Allowing oneself to mourn losses and seeking support from others who understand and validate their feelings.

Creating Legacies: Reflecting on and documenting personal legacies, stories, and values to leave behind for future generations.

Loss of Independence

Physical Decline:

Health Challenges: Aging may bring physical ailments, chronic conditions, or disabilities that limit mobility, independence, and daily activities.

Coping Mechanisms:

Adaptive Strategies: Utilizing assistive devices, home modifications, or rehabilitation services to maintain independence and quality of life.

Acceptance and Adjustment: Adjusting expectations and focusing on what can be controlled or improved in terms of health and daily routines.

Social and Role Changes:

Dependency on Others: Increasing reliance on caregivers, family members, or community services for support and assistance.

Coping Mechanisms:

Building Support Networks: Cultivating strong relationships with caregivers, friends, and community members to alleviate feelings of isolation and dependence.

Maintaining Social Connections: Participating in social activities, clubs, or groups that provide opportunities for engagement and social interaction.

General Coping Strategies for Aging Sorrow

Open Communication: Talking openly with loved ones, caregivers, or healthcare professionals about fears, concerns, and emotional struggles associated with aging.

Engagement in Meaningful Activities: Pursuing hobbies, interests, and lifelong learning opportunities that foster a sense of purpose and fulfillment.

Physical and Mental Well-being: Prioritizing physical health through regular exercise, nutritious eating, adequate sleep, and managing stress effectively.

Seeking Professional Support: Consulting with therapists, counselors, or geriatric specialists who can provide emotional support, guidance, and resources tailored to the challenges of aging.

Embracing Transitions: Embracing life transitions with resilience and adaptability, recognizing that change is a natural part of the aging process.

Conclusion

The sorrow of aging is a complex emotional journey that involves confronting mortality, adjusting to physical limitations, and navigating changes in independence and social roles. By acknowledging these challenges and utilizing effective coping strategies, individuals can cultivate resilience, maintain a sense of purpose, and find meaning in their lives despite the inevitable changes that come with aging.

Gender differences in experiencing and expressing sorrow

Gender differences in experiencing and expressing sorrow can vary due to a combination of biological, social, and cultural factors. While these differences are not absolute and can vary widely among individuals, here are some general patterns and considerations:

Experiencing Sorrow

Emotional Expression:

Women: Research suggests that women often tend to express sorrow more openly and verbally. They may seek social support and engage in discussions about their feelings more readily than men.

Men: Men may be more likely to internalize their sorrow or express it through actions rather than words. This can lead to behaviors such as withdrawal, distraction through work or hobbies, or engaging in solitary activities to process emotions.

Coping Styles:

Women: Females often use relational coping strategies, focusing on emotional processing and seeking support from friends and family. They may discuss their feelings, seek advice, or engage in activities that promote emotional healing.

Men: Males may employ more problem-focused coping strategies, aiming to solve practical issues related to their sorrow. They may also turn to solitary activities or distractions as a way to manage their emotions.

Cultural and Social Influences

Socialization:

Traditional Gender Roles: Societal norms and expectations often shape how men and women are taught to express and manage emotions. Women may be encouraged to be more emotionally expressive and nurturing, while men may be socialized to suppress emotions like sorrow to maintain a sense of stoicism and strength.

Cultural Differences: Cultural backgrounds can influence gender norms related to emotional expression. For example, cultures that emphasize collectivism and interdependence may encourage more open emotional expression regardless of gender.

Stigma and Perceptions:

Men: There can be a stigma associated with men expressing vulnerability or sadness, as it may be viewed as a sign of weakness. This can influence how men perceive and choose to express their sorrow, often leading to internalization or masking of emotions.

Women: While women may feel more socially accepted in expressing sorrow openly, they can also face stereotypes or expectations that label them as overly emotional or sensitive.

Biological and Psychological Factors

Hormonal Influences: Biological differences in hormonal profiles, such as estrogen and testosterone levels, may contribute to variations in how emotions, including sorrow, are experienced and expressed.

Psychological Differences: Differences in cognitive and emotional processing between genders can impact how individuals interpret and respond to sorrowful situations. These differences can be influenced by factors such as personality traits, past experiences, and coping mechanisms learned over time.

Implications and Considerations

Support and Understanding: Recognizing these gender differences can help in providing appropriate support and understanding to individuals experiencing sorrow. Tailoring interventions and communication styles based on individual preferences and needs can promote effective coping and emotional well-being.

Breaking Stereotypes: Encouraging open dialogue and challenging gender stereotypes can create a more inclusive environment where individuals of all genders feel empowered to express and manage their emotions authentically.

In summary, while gender differences in experiencing and expressing sorrow exist, they are influenced by a complex interplay of biological, social, and cultural factors. Understanding these differences can foster empathy, support effective coping strategies, and promote emotional resilience across diverse individuals and communities.

CHAPTER FOUR

The Role of Culture and Society

Cultural attitudes towards sorrow and mourning practices

Cultural attitudes towards sorrow and mourning practices vary widely across different societies and can profoundly influence how individuals experience and express grief. Here's an exploration of some common cultural perspectives and practices related to sorrow and mourning:

Cultural Attitudes towards Sorrow

Expression of Emotions:

Western Cultures: In many Western cultures, there is often an expectation for individuals to openly express their emotions, including sorrow and grief. Talking about feelings, attending funerals, and seeking social support are commonly accepted practices.

Eastern Cultures: In contrast, some Eastern cultures may emphasize stoicism and restraint in expressing sorrow. Individuals may prioritize maintaining composure and may find solace in private rituals or meditation rather than public displays of emotion.

Duration and Acceptance:

Temporal Perspective: Cultural attitudes can influence how long sorrow is considered appropriate or acceptable. Some cultures have specific mourning periods or rituals that guide the duration and expression of grief.

Acceptance of Grief: In cultures where sorrow is openly acknowledged and accepted, individuals may feel more supported and less stigmatized in expressing their emotions.

Spiritual and Religious Beliefs:

Afterlife Beliefs: Cultural and religious beliefs about the afterlife often shape attitudes towards death and mourning. Beliefs in reincarnation, heaven, or spiritual continuance may provide comfort and a sense of continuity beyond physical loss.

Rituals and Ceremonies: Rituals such as prayers, offerings, and ceremonies performed for the deceased vary widely across cultures. These practices can help mourners feel connected to their cultural heritage and provide structure for processing grief.

Mourning Practices

Funeral and Burial Customs:

Burial vs. Cremation: Cultural norms dictate whether individuals are buried or cremated after death. These practices can reflect religious beliefs, environmental considerations, and cultural traditions.

Funeral Ceremonies: Rituals surrounding funerals often involve specific prayers, speeches, music, and symbolic actions (e.g., placing flowers, offerings) that honor the deceased and provide comfort to the bereaved.

Community and Social Support:

Role of Community: In many cultures, mourning is a communal experience involving extended family, neighbors, and community members. This collective support can help alleviate sorrow and strengthen social bonds.

Social Customs: Customs such as bringing food to grieving families, visiting the bereaved, or holding memorial services serve as expressions of solidarity and compassion.

Memorialization and Remembrance:

Permanent Memorials: Cultural practices may include creating permanent memorials such as gravestones, plaques, or gardens to honor and remember the deceased.

Annual Commemorations: Some cultures observe annual rituals or festivals to commemorate the lives of loved ones, marking important anniversaries and ensuring they are not forgotten.

Cultural Variations and Adaptations

Globalization and Hybridization: In an increasingly interconnected world, cultural attitudes towards sorrow and mourning practices may evolve or blend as individuals and communities integrate diverse traditions and beliefs.

Migration and Diaspora: Cultural practices related to sorrow and mourning can change when individuals or communities relocate to new environments. This may lead to adaptations or syncretism of rituals to maintain cultural identity while adapting to local customs.

Implications for Support and Understanding

Understanding cultural attitudes towards sorrow and mourning practices is essential for providing culturally sensitive support to individuals and communities experiencing grief. Respect for diverse customs and beliefs fosters empathy, facilitates healing, and strengthens social cohesion during times of loss and sorrow. Embracing cultural diversity in mourning practices enriches our understanding of human resilience and the universal need for compassion in times of grief.

The influence of religion and spirituality on the perception of sorrow

Religion and spirituality play significant roles in shaping how individuals perceive and experience sorrow. These influences vary widely across different religious and spiritual traditions, but several common themes and impacts can be identified:

Perspective on Suffering and Loss

Meaning-making and Purpose:

Religious Beliefs: Many religions provide frameworks for understanding suffering and sorrow within a broader context of divine purpose or cosmic order. Concepts such as karma (in Hinduism and Buddhism) or God's will (in Christianity and Islam) can offer explanations for why sorrow occurs and its significance in the spiritual journey.

Spiritual Growth: Sorrow may be viewed as an opportunity for spiritual growth, introspection, and developing virtues such as compassion, patience, and resilience.

Afterlife and Eternal Perspective:

Belief in Afterlife: Beliefs in an afterlife, reincarnation, or spiritual continuation beyond death can provide comfort by suggesting that sorrow is temporary and that reunion with loved ones is possible.

Healing and Redemption: Religious teachings often emphasize forgiveness, redemption, and the possibility of finding solace through faith and spiritual practices.

Coping Mechanisms and Rituals

Prayer and Meditation:

Communication with the Divine: Prayer and meditation are central practices in many religions. They provide channels for expressing sorrow, seeking guidance, and finding solace in a higher power or spiritual presence.

Mindfulness and Contemplation: Spiritual practices encourage individuals to engage in mindfulness and contemplation, which can help manage emotional distress and promote inner peace.

Rituals and Ceremonies:

Funeral and Mourning Rituals: Religious traditions often prescribe specific rituals and ceremonies to honor the deceased and support the grieving process. These rituals can include prayers, readings from sacred texts, symbolic gestures, and communal gatherings.

Community Support: Participation in religious rituals fosters a sense of community and shared purpose, providing social support and solidarity during times of sorrow.

Moral and Ethical Guidance

Ethical Frameworks:

Guidance on Virtues: Religious teachings often emphasize virtues such as compassion, empathy, and altruism, which guide how individuals respond to their own sorrow and the suffering of others.

Sense of Duty: Beliefs in ethical responsibilities towards family, community, and the broader world can provide a sense of purpose and direction in coping with sorrow.

Challenges and Questions of Faith

Spiritual Crisis:

Questioning Beliefs: Sorrow and loss can provoke existential questions about the nature of suffering, the fairness of life, and the existence of a benevolent higher power.

Seeking Meaning: Individuals may experience periods of doubt or spiritual crisis as they grapple with the implications of sorrow within their religious framework.

Integration and Cultural Context

Diversity of Beliefs: Religious and spiritual responses to sorrow vary greatly across cultures and denominations. Practices may adapt over time and in different geographical contexts, reflecting cultural diversity and evolving interpretations of sacred texts.

Interfaith Dialogue: Increasingly, interfaith dialogue explores common ground and shared values in addressing universal experiences of sorrow and loss. This dialogue fosters mutual understanding and collaboration in supporting individuals from diverse religious backgrounds.

Conclusion

Religion and spirituality profoundly influence how individuals perceive, cope with, and find meaning in sorrow. They provide frameworks for understanding suffering within larger cosmic or divine contexts, offer rituals and practices for grieving, and guide ethical responses to personal and communal sorrow. Understanding these influences can help caregivers, counselors, and communities provide culturally sensitive support to individuals navigating grief within their religious or spiritual beliefs.

Media representation of sorrow and its impact on societal norms

The media plays a significant role in shaping societal norms and perceptions, including how sorrow is represented and understood. Here's an exploration of the media's representation of sorrow and its impact on societal norms:

Media Representation of Sorrow

Portrayal in Fiction and Entertainment:

Movies, TV Shows, and Literature: Fictional narratives often depict characters experiencing profound sorrow due to personal losses, tragedies, or challenges. These portrayals can range from realistic and nuanced to sensationalized or melodramatic.

Character Archetypes: Media frequently portrays specific archetypes of sorrow, such as the grieving widow, the tormented hero, or the broken-hearted lover. These representations shape audience expectations and emotional responses to sorrow.

News Coverage and Real-life Events:

Reporting on Tragedies: Media coverage of real-life events, such as natural disasters, accidents, or acts of violence, often includes stories of sorrow and grief among affected individuals and communities.

Human Interest Stories: Personal narratives of individuals facing adversity or loss can evoke empathy and raise awareness about the emotional toll of sorrow in society.

Social Media and Digital Platforms:

User-generated Content: Platforms like social media enable individuals to share personal experiences of sorrow and grief publicly. These narratives can influence public discourse and mobilize support for social causes related to mental health and emotional well-being.

Memorialization and Virtual Communities: Online platforms provide spaces for memorialization, tribute pages, and virtual support groups where individuals can express sorrow, share memories, and find solidarity with others facing similar experiences.

Impact on Societal Norms

Normalization and Recognition:

Increasing Awareness: Media representation of sorrow can raise awareness about the diversity of human experiences and the universality of grief. It helps normalize discussions about emotional struggles and encourages empathy towards others' pain.

Reducing Stigma: By portraying sorrow and mental health challenges openly, media can contribute to reducing stigma associated with seeking help for emotional distress or grief-related issues.

Cultural and Emotional Literacy:

Shaping Cultural Norms: Media representations contribute to shaping cultural norms around how sorrow is expressed, managed, and supported within communities. They influence societal attitudes towards grief and mourning practices.

Educational Value: Thoughtful and accurate portrayals of sorrow in media can educate the public about healthy coping strategies, available resources, and the importance of social support in times of loss.

Critique and Sensationalism:

Stereotypes and Misrepresentation: Media can sometimes perpetuate stereotypes or sensationalize sorrow for dramatic effect, potentially trivializing or misrepresenting the emotional complexities of grief.

Impact on Mental Health: Unrealistic or overly dramatic portrayals of sorrow in media can inadvertently contribute to misinformation or misunderstandings about mental health issues, affecting how individuals perceive their own emotional struggles.

Media Ethics and Responsibility

Ethical Reporting and Sensitivity:

Balanced Coverage: Journalistic ethics emphasize the importance of sensitivity and respect when reporting on sorrowful events. Ethical guidelines encourage journalists to consider the impact of their coverage on individuals and communities affected by grief.

Avoiding Exploitation: Media professionals strive to avoid exploiting personal sorrow or sensationalizing tragedies purely for commercial gain, respecting the dignity and privacy of those experiencing grief.

Diverse Representation and Inclusivity:

Representation Matters: Media diversity initiatives seek to amplify voices and experiences of marginalized communities, including their experiences of sorrow and resilience. Diverse representation helps challenge stereotypes and enriches public understanding of cultural variations in grief and mourning practices.

Conclusion

The media's representation of sorrow influences societal norms by shaping perceptions, attitudes, and behaviors towards grief and emotional distress. Responsible and empathetic portrayals can foster greater cultural and emotional literacy, promote empathy, and encourage supportive responses within communities. However, media professionals and consumers alike should critically engage with representations of sorrow to ensure they are respectful, accurate, and contribute positively to public discourse on mental health and emotional well-being.

The stigma surrounding sorrow and mental health

The stigma surrounding sorrow and mental health issues is a complex societal issue rooted in various factors, including cultural beliefs, historical perspectives, and media influence. Here's an exploration of the stigma specifically related to sorrow and mental health:

Nature of Stigma

Misconceptions and Stereotypes:

Weakness or Character Flaw: There is a persistent belief in many societies that experiencing sorrow or struggling with mental health challenges signifies weakness or a personal character flaw.

Lack of Understanding: Limited understanding of the complexities of grief and mental health can lead to stereotypes that oversimplify or trivialize these experiences.

Fear and Avoidance:

Fear of Judgment: Individuals experiencing sorrow or mental health issues may fear judgment, rejection, or social ostracism if they disclose their feelings or seek help.

Stigmatizing Language: Stigmatizing language and derogatory terms used to describe people with mental health conditions contribute to negative perceptions and societal attitudes.

Cultural and Societal Factors

Cultural Beliefs and Traditions:

Stoicism vs. Emotional Expression: Cultural norms vary in terms of how openly individuals are encouraged to express sorrow or emotional distress. In some cultures, stoicism and emotional restraint may be valued over emotional vulnerability and seeking support.

Religious Beliefs: Religious teachings and cultural practices can influence attitudes towards sorrow and mental health, either supporting or hindering acceptance and understanding.

Historical Context and Media Influence:

Media Portrayals: Historical and contemporary media representations of sorrow and mental health can perpetuate stereotypes, sensationalize issues, or contribute to misunderstanding.

Public Perception: Negative portrayals in media can reinforce stigma and shape public opinion, impacting how individuals view themselves and others experiencing sorrow or mental health challenges.

Consequences of Stigma

Barriers to Help-Seeking:

Delayed Treatment: Stigma often discourages individuals from seeking timely and appropriate help for sorrow or mental health issues, leading to delayed intervention and potential worsening of symptoms.

Self-Stigma: Internalized stigma can lead individuals to feel ashamed or unworthy of support, exacerbating feelings of isolation and hindering recovery.

Impact on Relationships and Employment:

Social Isolation: Fear of stigma may lead individuals to withdraw from social interactions, affecting relationships and support networks.

Discrimination: Stigma can also manifest as discrimination in educational, employment, and healthcare settings, limiting opportunities and access to resources for individuals affected by sorrow or mental health conditions.

Addressing Stigma

Education and Awareness:

Promoting Understanding: Education campaigns and initiatives aimed at increasing public awareness about sorrow, grief, and mental health can challenge stereotypes and foster empathy.

Media Literacy: Encouraging critical engagement with media representations of sorrow and mental health helps mitigate harmful stereotypes and misinformation.

Advocacy and Support:

Community Support: Building supportive communities and peer networks where individuals can share experiences and seek validation without fear of judgment.

Policy and Legal Protections: Advocating for policies that protect individuals from discrimination based on mental health status and promote equitable access to healthcare and support services.

Changing Cultural Norms

Cultural Competence: Training healthcare providers and community leaders in cultural competence to better understand and address diverse beliefs and attitudes towards sorrow and mental health.

Promoting Inclusivity: Creating inclusive environments where individuals feel safe and supported in expressing their emotions and seeking help without stigma or discrimination.

Conclusion

Addressing the stigma surrounding sorrow and mental health requires a multifaceted approach that includes education, awareness, advocacy, and policy change. By challenging misconceptions, promoting empathy, and fostering supportive environments, societies can work towards reducing stigma and improving the well-being of individuals affected by sorrow and mental health challenges.

CHAPTER FIVE

Sorrow in Literature and Art

Sorrow as a theme in classical and modern literature

Sorrow, as a theme, has been a central motif in literature across various periods, from classical works to modern novels and poetry. It serves as a powerful tool for exploring the human condition, relationships, and existential questions. Here's an exploration of how sorrow has been depicted and explored in classical and modern literature:

Classical Literature

Greek Tragedy (e.g., Sophocles, Euripides):

Depiction of Fate and Tragedy: Greek tragedies often revolve around characters facing profound sorrow due to fate, often involving themes of loss, betrayal, and mortality.

Catharsis: Sorrow in Greek tragedy aims to evoke catharsis in the audience, allowing them to experience intense emotions vicariously and reflect on the inevitability of suffering in life.

Shakespearean Tragedies (e.g., "Hamlet", "King Lear"):

Human Frailty and Conflict: Shakespeare's tragedies delve into the depths of human sorrow caused by betrayal, family discord, and existential angst.

Exploration of Grief: Characters like Hamlet and Lear grapple with profound sorrow over loss—of loved ones, power, or personal identity—highlighting the universal nature of grief and its transformative effects.

Modern Literature

19th and 20th Century Novels (e.g., Tolstoy, Dickens):

Social Realism and Emotional Depth: Authors like Leo Tolstoy and Charles Dickens explored sorrow in the context of societal injustices, personal tragedies, and moral dilemmas.

Psychological Realism: Characters' inner lives and emotional turmoil are often portrayed with psychological depth, depicting sorrow as a complex emotion rooted in personal and social contexts.

Existentialist Literature (e.g., Camus, Sartre):

Absurdity and Alienation: Existentialist writers like Albert Camus and Jean-Paul Sartre examined sorrow through the lens of existential despair, reflecting on the absurdity of life and the inevitability of suffering.

Individual Isolation: Characters often experience sorrow stemming from existential isolation, grappling with the meaninglessness of existence and the search for personal authenticity.

Contemporary Fiction and Poetry:

Identity and Loss: Modern authors and poets continue to explore sorrow in the context of identity, loss of innocence, and fractured relationships.

Diverse Perspectives: Literature today often embraces diverse voices and experiences of sorrow, addressing issues such as grief, trauma, displacement, and social injustice.

Themes and Symbolism

Loss and Bereavement: Sorrow often revolves around the experience of losing loved ones or grappling with the inevitability of death.

Isolation and Alienation: Characters frequently confront sorrow stemming from feelings of loneliness, disconnection, or estrangement from society or oneself.

Redemption and Transformation: Sorrow can also serve as a catalyst for personal growth, moral reflection, and the pursuit of redemption or reconciliation.

Conclusion

Sorrow in literature serves as a timeless theme that resonates with readers by capturing the complexity of human emotions and experiences. Whether depicted in classical tragedies, modern novels, or contemporary poetry, sorrow offers insights into the universal struggles of individuals facing adversity, loss, and existential dilemmas. Through literature, readers can empathize with characters' journeys, reflect on their own emotions, and contemplate the deeper meanings of sorrow in the human experience.

Representation of sorrow in visual arts and music

Sorrow, as an emotional theme, has been expressed profoundly in visual arts and music throughout history. Artists and musicians have used these mediums to capture the depth of human suffering, grief, and melancholy, often conveying universal emotions that resonate across cultures and time periods.

Representation in Visual Arts

Depiction of Grief and Tragedy:

Historical Context: In classical art, sorrow was often depicted through mythological scenes, religious narratives, or historical events that conveyed themes of loss, martyrdom, or lamentation.

Visual Symbolism: Artists employed symbols such as dark colors, dramatic lighting, weeping figures, and expressive gestures to evoke sorrow and emotional intensity.

Portraits of Sorrow:

Faces of Emotion: Portraits often captured the nuances of sorrow through facial expressions, body language, and subtle details that convey inner turmoil and melancholy.

Personal and Collective Grief: Artists portrayed individual sorrow as well as collective grief, such as during times of war, natural disasters, or societal upheaval.

Symbolism and Allegory:

Memento Mori: Symbolism like skulls, wilted flowers, or clocks (representing the passage of time) often reminded viewers of mortality and the transience of life, evoking sorrowful contemplation.

Allegorical Representations: Allegories of sorrow, such as the figure of the "weeping woman" or "mourning mother," were common in art to symbolize universal human suffering.

Examples in Music

Classical Music and Opera:

Emotional Depth: Composers like Johann Sebastian Bach, Wolfgang Amadeus Mozart, and Ludwig van Beethoven explored sorrow through compositions that expressed grief, longing, and spiritual anguish.

Operatic Tragedies: Operas such as Giuseppe Verdi's "La traviata" or Giacomo Puccini's "Madama Butterfly" portrayed characters experiencing profound sorrow and emotional turmoil.

Romanticism and Expressionism:

Intense Emotions: Romantic composers like Frédéric Chopin and Gustav Mahler used music to convey deep emotional states, including sorrow, through melodic richness, harmonic complexity, and dynamic contrasts.

Expressionist Works: In the 20th century, composers like Arnold Schoenberg and Alban Berg embraced atonal and dissonant music to express existential angst and psychological sorrow.

Folk and Blues Traditions:

Authenticity and Raw Emotion: Folk music traditions, such as American blues or British folk ballads, often conveyed sorrow through raw, emotive lyrics and melodies that spoke to personal hardships and societal injustices.

Catharsis and Resilience: These musical genres provided a means for individuals to express and cope with sorrow while also fostering a sense of communal solidarity and resilience.

Cross-Cultural Perspectives

Traditional and Indigenous Art:

Rituals and Ceremonies: Indigenous cultures around the world incorporate visual arts and music into rituals and ceremonies that address sorrow, loss, and healing within communal contexts.

Symbolic Representation: Art forms like Aboriginal dot paintings, African masks, or Japanese Noh theater incorporate symbolic elements that represent sorrow and catharsis through cultural lenses.

Contemporary Art and Music:

Exploration of Modern Issues: Contemporary artists and musicians continue to explore themes of sorrow in response to contemporary issues such as global conflicts, environmental degradation, and social inequalities.

Multimedia and Technology: Advancements in multimedia art and digital music production have expanded the ways in which sorrow can be represented and experienced through interactive and immersive installations.

Conclusion

Sorrow in visual arts and music serves as a profound vehicle for human expression, allowing artists and musicians to convey the complexities of grief, loss, and emotional turmoil. Across different cultures and historical periods, these mediums have provided catharsis, reflection, and empathy for individuals grappling with sorrowful experiences. Whether through poignant portraits, emotive musical compositions, or symbolic representations, visual arts and music continue to offer poignant insights into the universal aspects of human suffering and resilience.

Therapeutic aspects of expressing sorrow through creative outlets

Expressing sorrow through creative outlets can be highly therapeutic, offering individuals a means to process emotions, gain insight, and promote healing. Here are some therapeutic aspects of expressing sorrow through creative activities:

1. Emotional Release and Catharsis

Outlet for Emotions: Creative outlets such as art, writing, music, or dance provide a safe space to release pent-up emotions associated with sorrow, allowing individuals to express themselves freely.

Cathartic Experience: Engaging in creative activities can lead to catharsis, a purging or cleansing of emotions, which can alleviate emotional distress and promote psychological well-being.

2. Self-Exploration and Insight

Processing Complex Feelings: Creativity encourages introspection and exploration of complex feelings associated with sorrow, helping individuals gain deeper insights into their emotions and experiences.

Symbolic Expression: Symbols, metaphors, and imagery used in creative works can represent inner conflicts, grief stages, or personal narratives, facilitating a deeper understanding of one's emotional landscape.

3. Sense of Control and Empowerment

Agency in Expression: Creative activities provide individuals with a sense of control over their sorrowful experiences, allowing them to shape and articulate their feelings in a meaningful way.

Empowerment: Through creativity, individuals can transform feelings of helplessness or despair into a proactive process of self-expression and personal empowerment.

4. Connection and Communication

Shared Experience: Creative expression can foster connection and empathy with others who may resonate with similar emotions or experiences of sorrow.

Non-Verbal Communication: For those who struggle to articulate their feelings verbally, creative outlets offer alternative forms of communication that are equally powerful and evocative.

5. Healing and Resilience Building

Promoting Healing: Engaging in creative activities can contribute to emotional healing by facilitating the integration of sorrowful experiences into one's personal narrative and promoting adaptive coping mechanisms.

Resilience Building: By expressing sorrow creatively, individuals develop resilience skills, such as emotional regulation, problem-solving, and coping strategies, which support long-term emotional well-being.

Examples of Creative Outlets for Expressing Sorrow

Visual Arts: Painting, drawing, sculpture, and photography can visually capture emotions, memories, or symbolic representations of sorrow.

Writing: Journaling, poetry, or storytelling allows individuals to articulate their thoughts and feelings, creating narratives that explore themes of loss, longing, or acceptance.

Music and Dance: Composing music, playing instruments, or engaging in dance can convey emotions through rhythm, melody, movement, and expression.

Crafts and DIY Projects: Activities such as knitting, woodworking, or gardening provide tactile and sensory experiences that promote mindfulness and relaxation while channeling emotions.

Considerations for Therapeutic Use

Safe Environment: Creating a supportive and non-judgmental environment is crucial for individuals to feel comfortable exploring and expressing their sorrow through creativity.

Professional Guidance: In some cases, working with a trained therapist or counselor who specializes in creative arts therapy can provide additional guidance and support in using creative outlets therapeutically.

Personalization: Tailoring creative activities to individual preferences and strengths enhances their therapeutic benefits, ensuring that the process feels meaningful and authentic.

By embracing creative outlets as a therapeutic tool for expressing sorrow, individuals can harness the healing power of creativity to navigate grief, promote emotional resilience, and embark on a journey of personal growth and healing.

Analysis of notable works that portray sorrow

Several notable works across literature, visual arts, and music vividly portray sorrow, delving deep into the complexities of human emotion and the universal experience of grief. Here's an analysis of some of these works:

Literature

"Hamlet" by William Shakespeare:

Theme of Grief and Revenge: Shakespeare's tragedy "Hamlet" explores profound sorrow through the protagonist, Hamlet, who mourns the death of his father and struggles with existential questions. The famous soliloquy "To be, or not to be" reflects Hamlet's inner turmoil and contemplation of mortality.

Emotional Turmoil: The play delves into themes of betrayal, loss, and familial conflict, portraying how sorrow can consume and drive individuals to drastic actions.

"The Bell Jar" by Sylvia Plath:

Personal and Existential Sorrow: Plath's semi-autobiographical novel captures the protagonist Esther Greenwood's descent into mental illness and deep sorrow. It explores themes of identity crisis, societal pressures, and the struggle for self-acceptance amidst personal anguish.

Psychological Depth: The novel portrays sorrow as a pervasive force that permeates every aspect of Esther's life, from her relationships to her sense of self-worth.

"The Road" by Cormac McCarthy:

Post-Apocalyptic Sorrow: McCarthy's novel depicts a father and son's journey through a post-apocalyptic landscape, where they confront sorrow and despair in the face of a bleak and desolate world.

Parental Love and Loss: The novel explores themes of parental love, survival, and the human spirit's resilience amidst overwhelming grief and hopelessness.

Visual Arts

"The Scream" by Edvard Munch:

Expressionist Anguish: Munch's iconic painting captures a figure in a moment of intense emotional distress, symbolizing existential dread and inner turmoil. The swirling colors and distorted forms evoke a sense of deep sorrow and despair.

Universal Symbolism: "The Scream" has become a universal symbol of existential angst and the human experience of profound sorrow and alienation.

"Guernica" by Pablo Picasso:

Political Sorrow and Protest: Picasso's mural masterpiece "Guernica" portrays the horrors of war and the sorrow inflicted upon innocent civilians during the bombing of Guernica in the Spanish Civil War.

Symbolic Imagery: The painting's fragmented forms and stark monochromatic palette convey the chaos, agony, and sorrow of war, serving as a powerful anti-war statement and a testament to human suffering.

Music

"Adagio for Strings" by Samuel Barber:

Musical Elegy: Barber's composition is renowned for its emotional depth and hauntingly beautiful melody, which evokes sorrow and mourning. It has been used in numerous contexts, including memorials and ceremonies, to express collective grief and reflection.

Cathartic Expression: The music builds gradually, conveying a sense of emotional release and catharsis, making it a poignant exploration of sorrow through orchestral music.

"Hurt" by Nine Inch Nails (covered by Johnny Cash):

Personal Reflection and Regret: Johnny Cash's cover of "Hurt" transforms Trent Reznor's song into a haunting reflection on aging, regret, and the passage of time. Cash's weathered voice lends authenticity to the sorrowful lyrics, creating a deeply moving portrayal of personal sorrow.

Artistic Evolution: The cover is seen as a testament to Cash's own life experiences, resonating with listeners on a profound level through its raw emotion and introspective lyrics.

Analysis

Universal Themes: These works explore sorrow as a universal human experience, transcending cultural and temporal boundaries to evoke empathy and introspection.

Medium-Specific Expressions: Literature, visual arts, and music each offer unique ways to depict sorrow, whether through narrative depth, visual symbolism, or musical composition.

Impact and Interpretation: The portrayal of sorrow in these works invites audiences to reflect on themes of loss, grief, resilience, and the human capacity for emotional expression and healing.

In summary, these notable works exemplify how artists across different mediums have captured and conveyed sorrow, enriching our understanding of this profound emotion and its significance in the human experience.

CHAPTER SIX

Coping Mechanisms and Healing

Psychological therapies and counseling for managing sorrow

Psychological therapies and counseling play crucial roles in helping individuals manage sorrow and navigate the complex emotions associated with grief and loss. Here are several therapeutic approaches commonly used in addressing sorrow:

1. Grief Counseling

Focus: Grief counseling focuses specifically on helping individuals process and cope with the emotional pain of loss.

Goals: Therapists aim to facilitate healthy grieving by validating emotions, providing emotional support, and guiding clients through the stages of grief (e.g., denial, anger, bargaining, depression, acceptance).

Techniques: Techniques may include storytelling, reminiscing, and exploring the meaning of the loss. Cognitive-behavioral strategies help clients challenge unhelpful thoughts and manage distressing emotions.

2. Cognitive Behavioral Therapy (CBT)

Focus: CBT helps individuals recognize and change negative thought patterns and behaviors that contribute to prolonged sorrow or difficulty coping with loss.

Goals: Therapists work with clients to identify and challenge cognitive distortions related to the loss, develop coping strategies for managing grief triggers, and gradually engage in activities that promote emotional healing.

Techniques: Techniques include cognitive restructuring, behavioral activation, relaxation training, and gradual exposure to grief-related stimuli.

3. Mindfulness-Based Therapies

Focus: Mindfulness-based approaches (e.g., Mindfulness-Based Stress Reduction, Acceptance and Commitment Therapy) help individuals develop present-moment awareness and acceptance of their grief-related emotions.

Goals: Therapists assist clients in cultivating non-judgmental awareness of sorrowful feelings, fostering self-compassion, and improving emotional regulation.

Techniques: Techniques involve mindfulness meditation, body scan exercises, and mindful movement practices to enhance emotional resilience and promote a sense of calm amidst grief.

4. Supportive Therapy

Focus: Supportive therapy provides a safe and empathetic space for individuals to express their sorrow, receive validation, and explore coping strategies.

Goals: Therapists offer emotional support, normalize grief reactions, and help clients strengthen their support networks.

Techniques: Techniques include active listening, empathy-building, psychoeducation about grief, and fostering a therapeutic alliance based on trust and understanding.

5. Interpersonal Therapy (IPT)

Focus: IPT focuses on how grief and loss impact interpersonal relationships and vice versa.

Goals: Therapists help clients identify and address interpersonal issues exacerbated by grief, such as changes in social roles, communication difficulties, or strained relationships.

Techniques: Techniques include role-playing, communication skills training, and exploring grief-related changes in relationships to improve social support and overall well-being.

6. Complicated Grief Therapy (CGT)

Focus: CGT is specifically designed for individuals experiencing prolonged and intense grief reactions that interfere with daily functioning.

Goals: Therapists help clients process and adaptively cope with grief, address feelings of emptiness or disbelief, and facilitate emotional acceptance and adjustment.

Techniques: Techniques may include narrative therapy, imaginal revisiting of the loss, and integrating memories of the deceased into a new life narrative.

Integrative Approaches and Considerations

Holistic Care: Integrative approaches may combine therapeutic techniques with complementary therapies such as art therapy, music therapy, or yoga to address emotional, physical, and spiritual dimensions of grief.

Cultural Sensitivity: Therapists should be culturally competent, respecting diverse beliefs and mourning practices that may influence how individuals experience and express sorrow.

Self-Care and Resilience: Therapy often includes education on self-care practices, resilience-building strategies, and ongoing support to help individuals navigate the grieving process over time.

Conclusion

Psychological therapies and counseling offer tailored interventions to support individuals experiencing sorrow and grief. By providing a safe space for emotional expression, offering coping strategies, and fostering resilience, therapists help clients navigate the complex and painful emotions associated with loss, ultimately promoting healing and adjustment to life without their loved one. Therapy can be instrumental in empowering individuals to find meaning and purpose in their lives while honoring the memory of those they have lost.

The role of mindfulness and meditation in alleviating sorrow

Mindfulness and meditation play significant roles in alleviating sorrow by providing individuals with tools to cultivate present-moment awareness, acceptance of difficult emotions, and a sense of inner peace. Here's how mindfulness and meditation contribute to managing sorrow:

1. Awareness and Acceptance

Present-Moment Focus: Mindfulness practices encourage individuals to anchor their awareness in the present moment, helping them observe their sorrowful thoughts and emotions without judgment.

Acceptance of Emotions: Instead of resisting or suppressing sorrow, mindfulness fosters an attitude of acceptance towards emotions, allowing individuals to acknowledge and experience them fully.

2. Emotional Regulation

Reducing Emotional Reactivity: Mindfulness meditation teaches techniques to respond to emotions calmly rather than react impulsively. This can help individuals manage the intensity of sorrowful feelings and prevent them from becoming overwhelming.

Enhancing Emotional Resilience: Regular practice of mindfulness can strengthen emotional resilience, enabling individuals to navigate grief and sorrow more effectively over time.

3. Cognitive Perspective

Challenging Negative Thought Patterns: Mindfulness practices, such as mindfulness-based cognitive therapy (MBCT), help individuals recognize and challenge negative thought patterns associated with sorrow, such as rumination or self-blame.

Promoting Psychological Flexibility: Meditation encourages a broader perspective on life's challenges, fostering psychological flexibility and adaptive coping strategies in the face of sorrow.

4. Stress Reduction and Relaxation

Physiological Benefits: Mindfulness and meditation techniques induce a relaxation response, reducing physiological symptoms of stress and promoting a sense of calmness.

Improving Sleep Quality: Chronic sorrow can disrupt sleep patterns. Mindfulness practices can improve sleep quality by calming the mind and reducing insomnia symptoms.

5. Spiritual and Existential Comfort

Connecting to Inner Wisdom: For some individuals, mindfulness and meditation provide opportunities to connect with deeper aspects of themselves or spiritual beliefs, offering comfort and solace during times of sorrow.

Finding Meaning and Purpose: Practices like loving-kindness meditation can cultivate feelings of compassion and connection, helping individuals find meaning in their sorrow and strengthen social bonds.

6. Integrative Healing

Complementary Therapies: Mindfulness and meditation can complement other therapeutic approaches, such as grief counseling or cognitive-behavioral therapy, by enhancing emotional regulation and resilience.

Long-Term Well-Being: Regular practice of mindfulness fosters long-term well-being by promoting self-awareness, self-compassion, and a sense of inner stability, which are essential in navigating the ongoing challenges of sorrow and grief.

Practical Application

Starting Small: Beginners can start with short mindfulness exercises, focusing on breath awareness or body scan techniques, gradually building up to longer meditation sessions.

Consistency: Regular practice is key to reaping the benefits of mindfulness and meditation in alleviating sorrow. Even brief daily sessions can have cumulative effects over time.

Professional Guidance: For individuals experiencing profound sorrow or complicated grief, seeking guidance from a trained mindfulness instructor or therapist specializing in mindfulness-based approaches can provide personalized support and guidance.

Conclusion

Mindfulness and meditation offer powerful tools for alleviating sorrow by promoting emotional awareness, acceptance, and resilience. These practices not only help individuals manage the immediate pain of grief but also foster long-term emotional well-being and a deeper sense of meaning in life. Integrating mindfulness into daily life can empower individuals to navigate sorrow with greater ease, finding moments of peace and connection amidst their grieving process.

Social support networks: family, friends, and support groups

Social support networks, encompassing family, friends, and support groups, play vital roles in helping individuals cope with sorrow and grief. Here's how each of these networks contributes to providing emotional support and resilience:

1. Family Support

Immediate and Intimate: Family members, such as parents, siblings, or children, often form the closest support network during times of sorrow.

Emotional Validation: Family provides emotional validation and a sense of belonging, acknowledging the depth of sorrow and validating the individual's feelings.

Practical Support: Family members can offer practical assistance with daily tasks, childcare, or household responsibilities, allowing grieving individuals time and space to process their emotions.

2. Friends and Peer Support

Social Companionship: Friends provide companionship and a sense of normalcy during a challenging time, offering opportunities for distraction and social engagement.

Listening and Empathy: Friends listen empathetically, offering non-judgmental support and understanding that can be crucial in validating feelings of sorrow.

Shared Activities: Engaging in shared activities or hobbies with friends can provide moments of joy and distraction from grief, promoting emotional well-being.

3. Support Groups and Community Networks

Shared Experience: Support groups bring together individuals who have experienced similar losses, providing a sense of solidarity and understanding.

Peer Validation: Interacting with others in support groups validates individual experiences of sorrow, reducing feelings of isolation and promoting emotional healing.

Expert Facilitation: Facilitated support groups led by trained professionals offer guidance and resources for coping with grief, providing psychoeducation and teaching coping strategies.

Benefits of Social Support Networks

Reducing Isolation: Sorrow can be isolating, but social support networks provide connections that combat loneliness and foster a sense of belonging.

Emotional Expression: Sharing feelings and memories with supportive individuals validates emotions and promotes emotional processing.

Practical Assistance: Support networks offer practical help with daily tasks, reducing stress and allowing individuals to focus on their emotional well-being.

Normalization of Grief: Interacting with others who understand grief normalizes the experience, validating emotions and reducing stigma.

Challenges and Considerations

Diverse Responses: Individuals within support networks may respond to grief differently, which can sometimes lead to misunderstandings or conflicts.

Changing Dynamics: Family and social dynamics may shift during grief, requiring open communication and adaptation to new roles and responsibilities.

Cultural Sensitivity: Cultural norms and expectations may influence how individuals seek and receive support, requiring sensitivity and respect for diverse beliefs and practices.

Seeking and Cultivating Support

Initiating Conversations: Open communication about needs and feelings encourages support from family and friends, fostering deeper connections.

Professional Guidance: In cases of complicated grief or significant emotional distress, seeking guidance from grief counselors or therapists can complement social support networks.

Self-Care: Balancing support from others with self-care practices, such as mindfulness or physical activity, promotes holistic well-being during the grieving process.

Conclusion

Social support networks—comprising family, friends, and support groups—are invaluable resources for individuals navigating sorrow and grief. They provide emotional validation, practical assistance, and opportunities for shared experiences that promote healing and resilience. By fostering connections and understanding within these networks, individuals can find strength and comfort as they journey through the complex emotions of grief.

Alternative and holistic approaches: yoga, acupuncture, and herbal remedies

Alternative and holistic approaches, such as yoga, acupuncture, and herbal remedies, offer diverse methods for individuals seeking to manage sorrow and promote emotional well-being. Here's an exploration of how these approaches can contribute to holistic care during times of grief:

1. Yoga

Mind-Body Connection: Yoga emphasizes the connection between mind and body through physical postures (asanas), breathing techniques (pranayama), and meditation.

Stress Reduction: Practicing yoga can reduce stress hormones like cortisol and promote relaxation, easing physical tension associated with sorrow.

Emotional Regulation: Yoga encourages mindfulness and self-awareness, helping individuals process emotions and cultivate resilience.

Community Support: Yoga classes provide social support and a sense of community, offering opportunities for shared experiences and mutual understanding among participants.

2. Acupuncture

Traditional Chinese Medicine: Acupuncture is based on the concept of balancing the flow of energy (qi) through pathways (meridians) in the body.

Pain Relief: Acupuncture sessions can help alleviate physical symptoms of grief, such as tension headaches or muscle stiffness, by stimulating specific points on the body.

Emotional Healing: Some individuals find acupuncture beneficial for addressing emotional imbalances and promoting a sense of calmness and well-being.

Individualized Treatment: Acupuncture treatments are often personalized to address the unique needs and symptoms of each individual experiencing grief.

3. Herbal Remedies

Natural Supplements: Herbal remedies, such as teas, tinctures, or supplements, may support emotional well-being and stress management during grief.

Adaptogenic Herbs: Adaptogens like ashwagandha or holy basil are believed to help the body adapt to stress and promote resilience.

Soothing Effects: Certain herbs, like chamomile or lavender, have calming properties that can aid in relaxation and sleep improvement.

Consultation: It's essential to consult with a qualified herbalist or healthcare provider before using herbal remedies, especially if taking medications or managing pre-existing health conditions.

Integration and Considerations

Complementary Approaches: Integrating alternative therapies with conventional treatments, such as psychotherapy or support groups, can enhance overall well-being and provide holistic support.

Personal Preferences: Individuals may have different preferences for alternative therapies based on cultural background, personal beliefs, or previous experiences.

Evidence-Based Practices: While these approaches offer potential benefits, evidence supporting their efficacy in grief management varies, and individual responses may differ.

Self-Care and Wellness Practices

Holistic Lifestyle: Beyond specific therapies, adopting a holistic approach to self-care—including healthy nutrition, regular physical activity, and adequate rest—supports emotional resilience during grief.

Mindfulness and Meditation: Combining alternative therapies with mindfulness practices can amplify their benefits, promoting emotional regulation and stress reduction.

Conclusion

Alternative and holistic approaches like yoga, acupuncture, and herbal remedies offer valuable tools for individuals seeking to manage sorrow and promote emotional well-being. These practices emphasize the interconnectedness of mind, body, and spirit, providing avenues for relaxation, emotional processing, and community support. While integrating these approaches into grief management can be beneficial, it's essential to approach them mindfully and in consultation with healthcare providers or qualified practitioners to ensure safety and effectiveness.

CHAPTER SEVEN

Sorrow in the Modern World

The impact of technology and social media on sorrow

The impact of technology and social media on sorrow is a complex and multifaceted issue, influencing how individuals experience, express, and cope with feelings of sadness and grief. Here's an exploration of both the positive and negative aspects:

Positive Impacts

Access to Support and Resources:

Online Communities: Social media platforms and online forums provide spaces for individuals to connect with others who may be experiencing similar sorrowful circumstances. This can reduce feelings of isolation and offer emotional support.

Information and Guidance: Technology allows quick access to resources such as grief counseling services, support groups, and self-help materials, which can aid individuals in coping with sorrow more effectively.

Expression and Awareness:

Personal Expression: Social media allows individuals to share their experiences of sorrow through personal stories, art, poetry, or blogs, fostering self-expression and validation of emotions.

Raising Awareness: Online campaigns and movements dedicated to raising awareness about mental health issues, grief, and bereavement can reduce stigma and promote understanding within broader communities.

Remote Connectivity:

Long-Distance Relationships: Technology facilitates communication and connection with loved ones who may be geographically distant, allowing for ongoing emotional support during times of sorrow.

Virtual Memorials: Platforms and websites enable the creation of virtual memorials or tribute pages, providing a digital space for honoring and remembering loved ones who have passed away.

Negative Impacts

Digital Overload and Distraction:

Information Overload: Constant exposure to sorrowful news, personal stories, or traumatic events on social media can overwhelm individuals and exacerbate feelings of sadness or anxiety.

Digital Distraction: Excessive use of technology as a distraction mechanism may hinder healthy coping strategies or delay emotional processing of grief and sorrow.

Comparison and Envy:

Social Comparison: Viewing idealized or curated portrayals of others' lives on social media can lead to feelings of inadequacy or envy, especially when comparing one's own sorrowful experiences to seemingly perfect lives online.

FOMO (Fear of Missing Out): Individuals experiencing sorrow may feel excluded or left out when seeing others' joyful experiences or milestones shared on social media, intensifying feelings of loneliness or isolation.

Impersonal Interactions:

Lack of Empathy: Digital communication often lacks the non-verbal cues and personal interactions present in face-to-face communication, potentially reducing the depth of emotional support and empathy offered.

Misinterpretation: Miscommunications or misunderstandings in online interactions can inadvertently exacerbate feelings of sorrow or contribute to interpersonal conflicts.

Ethical and Practical Considerations

Privacy and Boundary Management: Maintaining boundaries and privacy online can protect individuals from intrusive or insensitive interactions related to their sorrowful experiences.

Digital Well-being Practices: Balancing digital engagement with offline activities, self-care, and mindfulness can help mitigate the negative impacts of technology on emotional well-being.

Critical Engagement: Developing critical thinking skills and awareness of how digital media influences perceptions and emotions can empower individuals to navigate sorrowful experiences in a healthier manner.

Conclusion

The impact of technology and social media on sorrow is a dynamic interplay of opportunities and challenges. While these platforms can facilitate support, awareness, and connectivity during times of sorrow, they also pose risks related to information overload, comparison, and impersonal interactions. Understanding these dynamics and employing mindful engagement strategies can help individuals harness the positive aspects of technology while mitigating its potential negative impacts on emotional well-being.

Global events and collective sorrow: natural disasters, wars, and pandemics

Global events such as natural disasters, wars, and pandemics can evoke collective sorrow on a massive scale, affecting individuals, communities, and societies worldwide. Here's an analysis of how these events contribute to collective sorrow and their impact on the human experience:

Natural Disasters

Loss of Life and Property:

Human Tragedy: Natural disasters like earthquakes, tsunamis, hurricanes, and wildfires often result in significant loss of life, displacement, and destruction of homes and infrastructure.

Collective Grief: Communities affected by natural disasters experience collective grief as they mourn the loss of loved ones and the disruption of their lives.

Psychological and Emotional Toll:

Trauma and Distress: Survivors may experience trauma, anxiety, and post-traumatic stress disorder (PTSD) due to the sudden and catastrophic nature of natural disasters.

Long-Term Effects: The emotional impact can extend beyond the immediate aftermath, affecting mental health, community cohesion, and recovery efforts.

Global Solidarity and Aid:

International Response: Natural disasters often prompt global solidarity and humanitarian aid efforts, with countries and organizations mobilizing resources to provide relief, support, and reconstruction assistance.

Symbolic Gestures: Expressions of sympathy, donations, and volunteerism demonstrate solidarity and support for affected communities worldwide.

Wars and Conflicts

Humanitarian Crises and Loss of Life:

Human Cost: Wars and armed conflicts result in profound sorrow through casualties, displacement, and the destruction of infrastructure and cultural heritage.

Generational Impact: The intergenerational transmission of trauma and sorrow can affect communities for decades, shaping collective memory and social cohesion.

Displacement and Refugees:

Forced Migration: Wars and conflicts often force millions of people to flee their homes, leading to displacement, separation from loved ones, and uncertainty about the future.

Loss of Identity: Refugees and displaced persons experience sorrow over the loss of their homes, livelihoods, and cultural connections, facing challenges in resettlement and integration.

Global Responses and Peace Efforts:

Diplomatic Initiatives: International organizations, governments, and NGOs work to facilitate peace negotiations, humanitarian aid, and long-term reconciliation efforts in conflict-affected regions.

Advocacy and Activism: Civil society movements and advocacy groups raise awareness about the human toll of wars and advocate for peacebuilding initiatives and conflict resolution strategies.

Pandemics

Loss of Lives and Health Impacts:

Global Health Crisis: Pandemics, such as COVID-19, result in widespread sorrow due to illness, loss of loved ones, and the strain on healthcare systems.

Grief and Bereavement: Families and communities experience profound sorrow and grief over the sudden and often preventable loss of lives.

Social Disruption and Economic Impact:

Disrupted Lives: Lockdowns, quarantines, and social distancing measures exacerbate feelings of isolation, loneliness, and anxiety, contributing to collective sorrow.

Economic Hardship: Job losses, financial insecurity, and disruptions to education and daily life further compound the emotional and psychological toll of the pandemic.

Global Collaboration and Health Interventions:

Vaccine Distribution and Research: International collaboration in vaccine development, distribution, and public health interventions aim to mitigate the impact of the pandemic and prevent future outbreaks.

Healthcare Workers and Frontline Heroes: Recognition and support for healthcare workers and essential workers demonstrate global solidarity and gratitude for their sacrifices during the pandemic.

Conclusion

Global events such as natural disasters, wars, and pandemics evoke collective sorrow by disrupting lives, causing loss of life, and triggering widespread emotional and psychological distress. While these events highlight the resilience and solidarity of communities and nations, they also underscore the importance of preparedness, empathy, and global cooperation in responding to and mitigating the impact of collective sorrow on a global scale.

The rise of mental health awareness and its effects on handling sorrow

The rise of mental health awareness has significantly impacted how individuals and societies handle sorrow and grief, emphasizing the importance of understanding, support, and proactive coping strategies. Here's an analysis of how increased awareness of mental health has influenced the handling of sorrow:

1. Reducing Stigma and Promoting Open Dialogue

Normalization of Grief: Mental health awareness campaigns have helped destigmatize feelings of sorrow and grief, encouraging individuals to openly discuss their emotions and seek support without fear of judgment.

Encouraging Help-Seeking Behavior: Increased awareness has prompted more people to recognize the signs of distress in themselves and others, leading to earlier intervention and access to mental health services.

2. Empowerment Through Education and Resources

Understanding Grief as a Normal Response: Education about grief and mental health has helped individuals understand that sorrow is a natural response to loss, validating their emotions and reducing feelings of isolation.

Access to Information and Support: Resources such as helplines, online forums, therapy services, and self-help materials provide individuals with tools and strategies to cope with sorrow and navigate the grieving process effectively.

3. Integration of Mental Health in Healthcare Systems

Holistic Approach to Care: Mental health awareness has promoted the integration of psychological support into healthcare settings, ensuring that individuals receive comprehensive care that addresses both their physical and emotional needs.

Training for Healthcare Providers: Healthcare professionals are increasingly trained to recognize and respond to mental health concerns, including grief and sorrow, enhancing the quality of care and support offered to patients and families.

4. Community Support and Peer Networks

Peer Support Groups: Awareness initiatives have led to the development of peer support groups and community networks where individuals experiencing sorrow can connect with others who share similar experiences.

Building Resilient Communities: Collective awareness fosters community resilience by encouraging empathy, mutual support, and proactive measures to address mental health challenges, including sorrow and grief.

5. Policy and Advocacy Efforts

Advocacy for Mental Health Services: Increased awareness has driven policy changes and advocacy efforts to improve access to mental health services, funding for research, and initiatives that promote mental well-being.

Public Campaigns and Initiatives: Awareness campaigns raise public consciousness about mental health issues, educate communities about effective coping strategies, and advocate for systemic changes that support individuals experiencing sorrow and grief.

Challenges and Considerations

Cultural and Societal Differences: Awareness efforts need to consider cultural beliefs and societal attitudes towards grief, ensuring that support services are culturally sensitive and inclusive.

Continued Education and Training: Sustained efforts in mental health education and training are necessary to address ongoing challenges in recognizing and supporting individuals experiencing sorrow and grief.

Conclusion

The rise of mental health awareness has transformed how sorrow and grief are handled within individuals and societies, promoting empathy, understanding, and proactive support. By reducing stigma, empowering individuals with knowledge and resources, and fostering community resilience, awareness initiatives play a crucial role in promoting mental well-being and enhancing the quality of life for those navigating the complexities of sorrow and grief.

Case studies of public figures and their experiences with sorrow

Public figures often experience sorrow and grief in highly visible ways, providing insights into how individuals in the public eye navigate personal loss and adversity. Here are a few case studies of notable public figures and their experiences with sorrow:

1. Princess Diana

Loss and Public Grief: Following her tragic death in 1997, Princess Diana's passing deeply affected millions worldwide. Her public funeral and the outpouring of grief highlighted the profound sorrow experienced not only by her family but also by admirers around the globe.

Impact on Mental Health Awareness: Diana's openness about her struggles with mental health issues, including depression and bulimia, helped destigmatize these conditions and encouraged conversations about emotional well-being.

2. Nelson Mandela

Personal Losses: Nelson Mandela, the anti-apartheid revolutionary and former President of South Africa, endured significant personal losses during his lifetime, including the imprisonment and death of family members due to political persecution.

Resilience and Leadership: Mandela's ability to channel personal sorrow into advocacy for reconciliation and social justice became a hallmark of his leadership. His forgiveness towards former adversaries symbolized his commitment to healing wounds caused by apartheid.

3. Michelle Obama

Personal Losses and Advocacy: Former First Lady Michelle Obama has spoken openly about the grief she experienced following the deaths of her father and close friends. Her memoir, "Becoming," explores how these losses shaped her personal growth and commitment to promoting mental health awareness.

Empathy and Resilience: Obama's advocacy for mental health initiatives and support for military families reflects her understanding of the importance of empathy and resilience in overcoming sorrow and adversity.

4. Tom Hanks

Publicly Acknowledged Sorrow: Actor Tom Hanks has publicly discussed his experience of sorrow and grief, particularly following the loss of close friends and colleagues, including filmmaker Nora Ephron.

Coping Mechanisms: Hanks has spoken about how acting and creative pursuits have served as therapeutic outlets for processing grief, highlighting the role of creativity in navigating personal sorrow.

5. Malala Yousafzai

Trauma and Resilience: Malala Yousafzai, the Pakistani activist for female education and the youngest Nobel Prize laureate, survived an assassination attempt by the Taliban in 2012. The traumatic experience and ongoing threats to her safety have shaped her advocacy for education and girls' rights.

Turning Sorrow into Activism: Yousafzai's resilience in the face of adversity has inspired millions worldwide. She continues to use her platform to advocate for social justice and empowerment, demonstrating how personal sorrow can fuel transformative activism.

Lessons and Insights

Visibility and Impact: Public figures often use their platforms to raise awareness about sorrow and grief, promoting empathy and understanding among their audiences.

Personal Growth and Advocacy: Many public figures transform their personal sorrow into opportunities for advocacy and social change, highlighting the resilience and transformative power of grief.

Role Models for Coping: By sharing their experiences, public figures can serve as role models for individuals facing similar challenges, demonstrating effective coping strategies and the importance of seeking support.

These case studies illustrate how public figures navigate and influence perceptions of sorrow and grief, contributing to broader conversations about mental health, resilience, and the human experience. Their experiences resonate with diverse audiences, fostering empathy and promoting supportive communities.

CHAPTER EIGHT

Finding Meaning and Growth through Sorrow

Philosophical perspectives on sorrow and existential growth

Philosophical perspectives on sorrow often delve into the existential dimensions of human experience, exploring how sorrow can be a catalyst for personal growth, reflection, and existential understanding. Here are several philosophical viewpoints on sorrow and its potential for existential growth:

1. Existentialist Perspective

Suffering as Intrinsic to Existence: Existentialism, as articulated by thinkers like Jean-Paul Sartre and Albert Camus, acknowledges that sorrow and suffering are inherent aspects of the human condition.

Search for Meaning: Sorrow prompts individuals to confront fundamental questions about existence, meaning, and the nature of human suffering.

Freedom and Responsibility: Existentialists emphasize personal responsibility in navigating sorrow and finding meaning amidst adversity, emphasizing the freedom to create one's own values and responses to sorrow.

2. Stoic Philosophy

Endurance and Resilience: Stoicism, with figures such as Seneca and Marcus Aurelius, advocates for developing inner resilience and maintaining equanimity in the face of sorrow.

Acceptance of Fate: Stoics encourage acceptance of what cannot be changed (fate), focusing instead on cultivating virtues such as courage, wisdom, and self-control.

Transforming Adversity: Sorrow is viewed as an opportunity for personal growth and moral development, fostering inner strength and virtue through adversity.

3. Buddhist Philosophy

Impermanence and Suffering: Central to Buddhist teachings is the recognition of impermanence (anicca) and the inevitability of suffering (dukkha) as universal truths.

Compassionate Response: Buddhism encourages a compassionate response to sorrow, both for oneself and others, fostering empathy and understanding.

Path to Enlightenment: Sorrow can serve as a catalyst for spiritual awakening and enlightenment, prompting individuals to seek liberation (nirvana) from the cycle of suffering.

4. Phenomenology

Lived Experience: Phenomenological philosophers, like Martin Heidegger and Maurice Merleau-Ponty, explore the lived experience of sorrow and its impact on one's subjective world.

Existential Angst: Sorrow is seen as part of existential angst, prompting individuals to confront the limits of human existence and the search for authenticity.

Meaning-Making: Phenomenology emphasizes how individuals construct meaning through their experiences of sorrow, highlighting the importance of subjective interpretation and lived narratives.

5. Humanistic Psychology

Personal Growth and Self-Actualization: Humanistic psychologists, such as Carl Rogers and Abraham Maslow, view sorrow as a potential catalyst for personal growth and self-actualization.

Integration of Experience: Sorrow prompts individuals to integrate challenging emotions and experiences into their personal narratives, fostering psychological growth and resilience.

Holistic Development: Humanistic psychology emphasizes the holistic development of individuals, acknowledging sorrow as part of a broader journey towards self-understanding and fulfillment.

Integration and Practical Application

Reflection and Contemplation: Philosophical perspectives encourage individuals to engage in reflection and contemplation about the meaning and significance of sorrow in their lives.

Existential Courage: Embracing sorrow with existential courage involves confronting difficult truths and uncertainties, while striving to cultivate resilience and inner strength.

Community and Dialogue: Engaging in philosophical discourse and sharing perspectives with others can provide support and foster deeper insights into the existential dimensions of sorrow.

Conclusion

Philosophical perspectives offer rich insights into how sorrow can be understood as a profound aspect of human existence, capable of fostering existential growth, resilience, and spiritual awakening. By exploring these perspectives, individuals can find meaning and purpose in their experiences of sorrow, transforming adversity into opportunities for personal and existential development.

Stories of resilience and transformation following sorrowful experiences

Stories of resilience and transformation following sorrowful experiences are powerful narratives that highlight the human capacity to endure, grow, and find meaning even in the face of profound loss or adversity. Here are a few examples of such stories:

1. Viktor Frankl - Man's Search for Meaning

Background: Viktor Frankl, a Holocaust survivor and psychiatrist, endured the horrors of Nazi concentration camps during World War II, including the loss of his family.

Resilience: Despite unimaginable suffering, Frankl developed his existential philosophy, emphasizing the importance of finding meaning in all forms of existence, even in the most brutal circumstances.

Transformation: His seminal work, "Man's Search for Meaning," has inspired millions worldwide, offering insights into the resilience of the human spirit and the potential for growth through suffering.

2. Nelson Mandela - Long Walk to Freedom

Background: Nelson Mandela, the former President of South Africa, spent 27 years in prison for his anti-apartheid activism, enduring separation from his family and harsh conditions.

Resilience: Mandela maintained a steadfast commitment to justice and reconciliation, advocating for peace and equality throughout his life.

Transformation: Following his release from prison, Mandela led efforts to dismantle apartheid peacefully, becoming a global symbol of resilience, forgiveness, and hope.

3. Malala Yousafzai - I Am Malala

Background: Malala Yousafzai, a Pakistani activist for female education, survived a Taliban assassination attempt in 2012 at the age of 15.

Resilience: Despite the attack and ongoing threats, Malala continued her advocacy for girls' education globally, becoming the youngest-ever Nobel Prize laureate in 2014.

Transformation: Her courage and determination have inspired millions, sparking a worldwide movement for girls' education and empowering young people to stand up against injustice.

4. Oprah Winfrey - The Oprah Winfrey Show

Background: Oprah Winfrey, a media mogul and philanthropist, overcame a challenging childhood marked by poverty, abuse, and trauma.

Resilience: Despite early setbacks, Winfrey pursued a career in media and eventually hosted "The Oprah Winfrey Show," becoming one of the most influential figures in television history.

Transformation: Through her platform, Winfrey has championed discussions on social issues, personal growth, and empowerment, inspiring millions to overcome adversity and pursue their dreams.

5. Nick Vujicic - Life Without Limits

Background: Nick Vujicic was born with tetra-amelia syndrome, a rare disorder characterized by the absence of all four limbs.

Resilience: Despite physical challenges and experiences of bullying and depression, Vujicic became a motivational speaker, author, and advocate for disability rights and mental health awareness.

Transformation: Through his foundation and speaking engagements worldwide, Vujicic spreads a message of hope, resilience, and embracing life's challenges with courage and determination.

Themes of Resilience and Transformation

Adversity as a Catalyst: These stories illustrate how adversity can serve as a catalyst for personal growth, resilience, and profound transformation.

Finding Meaning: Individuals often find meaning in their experiences of sorrow by advocating for social justice, promoting education, or inspiring others through their stories.

Impact on Others: Resilient individuals often create ripple effects, empowering communities and inspiring collective action towards positive change.

Conclusion

Stories of resilience and transformation following sorrowful experiences exemplify the strength of the human spirit and the capacity for growth and renewal even in the most challenging circumstances. These narratives not only inspire hope but also remind us of the profound resilience that lies within each of us, encouraging empathy, compassion, and a shared commitment to overcoming adversity with courage and grace.

Strategies for finding meaning and purpose in the midst of sorrow

Finding meaning and purpose in the midst of sorrow is a deeply personal and transformative journey. While each individual's path is unique, here are several strategies that can help navigate this process:

1. Reflect on Values and Beliefs

Self-Exploration: Take time to reflect on your core values, beliefs, and what matters most to you. Clarifying your personal philosophy can provide a foundation for finding meaning amidst sorrow.

Meaning-Making: Consider how your experiences of sorrow fit into your broader life narrative. Reflect on past challenges you have overcome and how they have shaped your identity and values.

2. Engage in Creative Expression

Artistic Outlets: Explore creative forms of expression such as writing, painting, music, or journaling. Creative activities can facilitate emotional processing and help articulate feelings of sorrow and resilience.

Storytelling: Share your story with trusted friends, family, or through artistic mediums. Sharing your experiences can foster connection, empathy, and a sense of purpose in helping others navigate similar challenges.

3. Seek Support and Connection

Community Involvement: Engage with supportive communities, whether through support groups, religious organizations, or volunteer work. Connecting with others who share similar experiences can provide comfort and validation.

Professional Guidance: Consider seeking guidance from therapists, counselors, or spiritual advisors who specialize in grief and loss. Professional support can offer tools and perspectives to navigate sorrow and find meaning.

4. Practice Gratitude and Mindfulness

Gratitude Journaling: Regularly write down things you are grateful for, even amidst sorrow. Practicing gratitude can shift focus towards positive aspects of life and foster resilience.

Mindfulness Meditation: Incorporate mindfulness practices into your daily routine to cultivate present-moment awareness and acceptance of difficult emotions. Mindfulness can help manage stress and enhance emotional well-being.

5. Embrace Spiritual or Philosophical Insights

Spiritual Practices: Draw strength from spiritual or religious beliefs that provide comfort and guidance during times of sorrow. Engage in prayer, meditation, or rituals that resonate with your spiritual beliefs.

Philosophical Reflection: Explore philosophical perspectives on sorrow, such as existentialism or stoicism, which emphasize finding meaning through personal responsibility, resilience, and acceptance of life's challenges.

6. Set Meaningful Goals and Intentions

Purposeful Action: Identify goals or activities that align with your values and contribute positively to your well-being or community. Setting intentions can provide direction and a sense of purpose during difficult times.

Service to Others: Consider how your experiences of sorrow can inspire acts of kindness or service to others. Helping others can provide a sense of fulfillment and contribute to a greater sense of purpose.

7. Acceptance and Growth

Embrace Emotions: Allow yourself to experience and process a range of emotions associated with sorrow. Acceptance of emotions is a crucial step towards healing and finding meaning.

Personal Growth: View challenges as opportunities for personal growth and resilience-building. Reflect on lessons learned and how you have grown stronger through your experiences of sorrow.

Conclusion

Finding meaning and purpose in the midst of sorrow is a gradual and evolving process that requires self-reflection, connection with others, and engagement in meaningful activities aligned with personal values. By integrating these strategies into your journey, you can navigate sorrow with resilience, cultivate a sense of purpose, and ultimately find deeper meaning in your experiences.

The concept of post-traumatic growth and its implications

Post-traumatic growth (PTG) refers to positive psychological changes that individuals may experience as a result of struggling with and overcoming significant adversity or trauma. It challenges the traditional view that trauma only leads to negative consequences (such as PTSD or other psychological disorders) by acknowledging that trauma can also catalyze personal growth, resilience, and psychological transformation. Here are key aspects and implications of the concept of post-traumatic growth:

Key Aspects of Post-Traumatic Growth:

Domains of Growth:

Personal Strength: Increased resilience, self-confidence, and ability to cope with adversity.

Appreciation of Life: Enhanced appreciation for life and a renewed sense of purpose or meaning.

Improved Relationships: Deeper and more meaningful connections with others, increased empathy, and compassion.

New Possibilities: Greater openness to new opportunities, personal goals, and perspectives on life.

Spiritual or Existential Growth: Development of spiritual beliefs, a greater sense of connection with the universe, or a deeper understanding of existential questions.

Process of Growth:

Cognitive Processing: Reflecting on the trauma and making sense of the experience, including reevaluating priorities and beliefs.

Emotional Regulation: Managing intense emotions associated with trauma and finding ways to cope effectively.

Behavioral Changes: Making proactive changes in behavior or lifestyle that promote growth and well-being.

Relational Changes: Strengthening relationships or forming new ones that provide support and understanding.

Individual Differences:

Post-traumatic growth is not universal and varies among individuals. Factors such as personality traits, social support, coping strategies, and the nature of the trauma itself influence the likelihood and extent of PTG.

Implications of Post-Traumatic Growth:

Enhanced Resilience: Individuals who experience PTG often demonstrate increased resilience in the face of future challenges or adversities.

Shift in Clinical Practices:

Mental health professionals increasingly recognize the importance of addressing not only trauma-related disorders (e.g., PTSD) but also facilitating opportunities for PTG.

Therapeutic approaches such as narrative therapy, mindfulness-based interventions, and existential or meaning-centered therapies are used to promote PTG.

Personal and Collective Narratives:

PTG challenges the narrative of trauma as purely negative, offering a more nuanced understanding that includes opportunities for personal growth and transformation.

Sharing stories of PTG can inspire hope and resilience within communities affected by trauma, fostering collective healing and empowerment.

Research and Education:

Ongoing research continues to explore the factors that contribute to PTG and its long-term implications for individuals and societies.

Education and awareness campaigns aim to promote resilience-building strategies and foster a culture that supports growth and well-being following adversity.

Ethical Considerations:

Recognizing PTG emphasizes the importance of respecting individuals' autonomy and agency in their healing journey.

Ethical considerations include ensuring trauma survivors have access to supportive resources and interventions that facilitate meaningful growth and recovery.

Conclusion:

Post-traumatic growth represents a paradigm shift in understanding how individuals can not only survive but thrive in the aftermath of trauma. By acknowledging the potential for growth and resilience, PTG offers hope and empowerment to those navigating difficult experiences, highlighting the transformative power of human resilience and the capacity for personal growth amidst adversity.

CHAPTER NINE

The Future of Sorrow

Predicting trends in the experience and expression of sorrow

Predicting trends in the experience and expression of sorrow involves understanding evolving societal attitudes, technological advancements, and cultural shifts that shape how individuals perceive, cope with, and express grief. Here are some potential trends to consider:

1. Increased Awareness and Acceptance

Destigmatization of Grief: Continued efforts to reduce stigma around mental health and emotional well-being may lead to greater acceptance and normalization of sorrowful emotions.

Public Discourse: More open discussions in media, literature, and online platforms could foster empathy and understanding, encouraging individuals to express their sorrow more freely.

2. Digital and Technological Influences

Online Support Networks: Expansion of online communities and virtual support groups may provide accessible platforms for individuals to share experiences of sorrow and seek emotional support.

Digital Memorials: Continued development of digital platforms for creating memorials and honoring loved ones may redefine traditional rituals of mourning and remembrance.

3. Personalized and Holistic Approaches

Customized Grief Support: Tailored approaches to grief counseling and therapy could emerge, focusing on individual needs, cultural backgrounds, and personal beliefs.

Integration of Wellness Practices: Incorporation of mindfulness, art therapy, and other holistic practices into grief support programs may promote healing and resilience.

4. Cultural and Diversity Considerations

Cultural Sensitivity: Recognition and respect for diverse cultural expressions of sorrow and mourning may become more prominent in global contexts.

Intersectional Approaches: Understanding how factors like race, gender identity, and socioeconomic status intersect with grief experiences could lead to more inclusive support services.

5. Artistic and Creative Outlets

Innovation in Creative Expression: Advancements in technology and multimedia platforms may inspire new forms of artistic expression for processing and communicating sorrow.

Public Engagement: Art installations, virtual reality experiences, and interactive exhibitions could engage communities in collective expressions of grief and healing.

6. Impact of Global Events

Resilience Building: Learning from collective responses to global crises such as pandemics, natural disasters, and humanitarian conflicts may shape future strategies for resilience and community support.

Environmental and Social Justice Movements: Increasing awareness of climate-related grief and socio-political upheavals may influence how societies collectively acknowledge and address sorrow stemming from systemic challenges.

Challenges and Considerations

Ethical Use of Technology: Balancing digital connectivity with privacy concerns and ethical considerations in virtual grief support services.

Cultural Sensitivity: Recognizing diverse cultural norms and practices related to grief and mourning to ensure respectful and inclusive support.

Continued Research and Education: Advancing knowledge in grief psychology, trauma-informed care, and bereavement support to meet evolving needs.

Conclusion

Predicting trends in the experience and expression of sorrow involves anticipating shifts in societal norms, technological innovations, and cultural dynamics that influence how individuals and communities navigate grief. By fostering empathy, embracing diversity, and integrating holistic approaches to support, societies can evolve towards more compassionate and inclusive responses to sorrowful experiences. Ongoing dialogue, research, and innovation will play crucial roles in shaping future trends in grief expression and healing practices.

The role of advancements in mental health treatments

Advancements in mental health treatments play a pivotal role in transforming how individuals cope with sorrow and other emotional challenges. Here's an exploration of their significance:

1. Improved Access and Delivery of Care

Teletherapy and Telepsychiatry: Advancements in technology have facilitated the widespread adoption of teletherapy and telepsychiatry services, allowing individuals to access mental health support remotely. This has been particularly beneficial during times of crisis or when in-person visits are not feasible.

Digital Mental Health Platforms: Mobile apps and online platforms offer tools for self-care, psychoeducation, and virtual support groups, enhancing accessibility and convenience for individuals seeking mental health resources.

2. Innovative Therapeutic Approaches

Psychotherapy Advancements: Therapeutic modalities such as cognitive-behavioral therapy (CBT), dialectical behavior therapy (DBT), and mindfulness-based interventions continue to evolve. Newer approaches integrate evidence-based practices with personalized treatment plans to address diverse needs and preferences.

Neuroscience and Psychopharmacology: Research in neuroscience has led to the development of novel medications and treatments targeting specific neurotransmitters and brain circuits implicated in mood disorders and trauma-related conditions.

3. Holistic and Integrative Care Models

Complementary and Alternative Therapies: Integrative approaches combine conventional mental health treatments with complementary therapies such as art therapy, yoga, and acupuncture, promoting holistic well-being and resilience.

Trauma-Informed Care: Recognition of the impact of trauma on mental health has prompted trauma-informed care models that prioritize safety, trustworthiness, and empowerment in therapeutic relationships.

4. Personalized Medicine and Precision Psychiatry

Genomic Research: Advances in genomic research and personalized medicine hold promise for identifying genetic markers and biological factors that influence mental health conditions, informing targeted treatment strategies.

Precision Psychiatry: Tailored interventions based on individual biomarkers, psychosocial factors, and treatment response profiles aim to optimize therapeutic outcomes and minimize adverse effects.

5. Collaborative Care and Community Integration

Integrated Healthcare Settings: Collaborative care models involving multidisciplinary teams (e.g., psychiatrists, psychologists, social workers, primary care providers) enhance coordination of mental health and medical services, improving overall health outcomes.

Community-Based Initiatives: Outreach programs, peer support networks, and community partnerships promote early intervention, resilience-building, and stigma reduction, fostering supportive environments for individuals experiencing sorrow and other mental health challenges.

Challenges and Considerations

Equity in Access: Disparities in access to mental health services based on socioeconomic status, geographic location, and cultural background require targeted efforts to ensure equitable care for all individuals.

Ethical and Cultural Sensitivity: Ethical considerations in the use of emerging technologies, genetic testing, and culturally competent care are essential to promoting trust and respect within diverse populations.

Research and Evidence-Based Practices: Continued investment in research, clinical trials, and outcome studies is crucial for validating new treatments, enhancing efficacy, and informing best practices in mental health care.

Conclusion

Advancements in mental health treatments have revolutionized the landscape of care for individuals experiencing sorrow and other emotional distress. By expanding access, integrating innovative therapies, and embracing personalized approaches, these advancements empower individuals to manage their mental health effectively, promote resilience, and enhance overall well-being. Continued collaboration, education, and advocacy are essential to furthering progress in mental health care and meeting the evolving needs of diverse populations globally.

Societal changes and their potential impact on sorrow

Societal changes can significantly impact how individuals experience and cope with sorrow, influencing cultural norms, support systems, and community responses. Here's an analysis of several societal changes and their potential effects on sorrow:

1. Changing Family Structures

Impact on Support Systems: Shifts towards nuclear families, single-parent households, and non-traditional family structures may alter traditional support networks for individuals experiencing sorrow.

Role Redefinition: Evolving roles and responsibilities within families could affect how grief is shared, processed, and supported across generations and family members.

2. Technological Advancements

Digital Communication: Increased reliance on digital platforms and social media for communication and social interaction may influence how individuals express and seek support for sorrow.

Virtual Memorials: Digital spaces for creating memorials and sharing memories may provide new avenues for collective mourning and remembrance.

3. Globalization and Mobility

Cultural Diversity: Exposure to diverse cultural practices and beliefs about grief may enrich perspectives on sorrow and mourning rituals, fostering cross-cultural understanding and empathy.

Transnational Families: Separation from family members due to migration or globalization may complicate grief experiences, requiring innovative ways to maintain connections and provide support.

4. Attitudes Towards Mental Health

Reducing Stigma: Increasing awareness and acceptance of mental health issues may encourage individuals to seek help for grief-related concerns, promoting earlier intervention and support.

Integration of Mental Health: Integration of mental health services into primary care and community settings may improve access to grief counseling and specialized support.

5. Social Movements and Advocacy

Collective Action: Social movements advocating for justice, human rights, and environmental sustainability may address systemic causes of sorrow, such as societal injustices and environmental crises.

Community Resilience: Activism and community engagement in response to collective grief can foster solidarity, resilience, and adaptive responses to adversity.

6. Healthcare and Aging Population

End-of-Life Care: Advances in palliative care and hospice services may enhance quality of life for individuals facing terminal illness and their families, providing compassionate support during end-of-life stages.

Aging Society: Demographic shifts towards an aging population may increase awareness of grief and loss associated with caregiving, chronic illness, and end-of-life transitions.

Challenges and Considerations

Digital Divide: Disparities in access to technology and digital literacy may limit the benefits of virtual support networks and online resources for grieving individuals, exacerbating feelings of isolation.

Cultural Sensitivity: Recognizing diverse cultural norms and beliefs about grief is essential to providing respectful and inclusive support services within multicultural societies.

Ethical Considerations: Ethical dilemmas in end-of-life care, genetic testing, and the use of emerging technologies require careful consideration to uphold dignity, autonomy, and cultural values.

Conclusion

Societal changes influence how sorrow is experienced, expressed, and supported within communities. By embracing diversity, reducing stigma around mental health, leveraging technological innovations, and promoting compassionate care practices, societies can foster resilience, empathy, and inclusive support systems for individuals navigating grief and loss. Continued dialogue, research, and advocacy are crucial to addressing evolving societal needs and promoting holistic approaches to grief and bereavement support.

Encouraging a more compassionate and understanding approach to sorrow

Encouraging a more compassionate and understanding approach to sorrow involves fostering empathy, providing support, and promoting open dialogue within communities. Here are several strategies to cultivate a compassionate and understanding response to sorrow:

1. Education and Awareness

Promote Mental Health Literacy: Increase public awareness about the normalcy of grief and the diversity of grief experiences. Education can help reduce stigma and encourage supportive attitudes towards those experiencing sorrow.

Provide Resources: Make information about grief support services, counseling, and community resources readily available. This empowers individuals to seek help and support when needed.

2. Normalize Expressions of Sorrow

Create Safe Spaces: Establish environments where individuals feel comfortable expressing their emotions without judgment or criticism. This could include workplaces, schools, community centers, and online forums.

Encourage Communication: Foster open and honest conversations about grief and loss. Encourage active listening and validation of emotions to create a supportive atmosphere.

3. Empathy and Active Support

Practice Empathetic Listening: Listen attentively to those experiencing sorrow without trying to fix their feelings. Validate their emotions and offer compassionate responses.

Offer Practical Assistance: Provide practical support such as helping with daily tasks, offering meals, or assisting with childcare. Small gestures can alleviate some of the burdens associated with grief.

4. Cultural Sensitivity and Diversity

Respect Cultural Practices: Recognize and respect diverse cultural norms and rituals related to grief and mourning. Avoid imposing one-size-fits-all approaches to supporting grieving individuals.

Include Everyone: Ensure inclusivity in grief support initiatives by considering the unique needs and experiences of marginalized communities, including LGBTQ+ individuals, immigrants, and people of different faiths.

5. Community and Social Support

Build Support Networks: Foster connections within communities through support groups, peer counseling programs, and volunteer networks dedicated to grief support.

Encourage Peer Support: Promote the role of peers and friends in providing emotional support. Peer support networks can offer understanding and solidarity during times of sorrow.

6. Advocacy and Policy

Advocate for Mental Health Services: Support policies and initiatives that improve access to mental health services, including grief counseling and therapy. Advocate for funding and resources to address mental health needs within communities.

Raise Awareness Through Advocacy: Participate in campaigns and advocacy efforts to raise awareness about the importance of compassionate responses to grief. Challenge stigma and promote empathy in public discourse.

Conclusion

Encouraging a more compassionate and understanding approach to sorrow involves collective efforts to foster empathy, provide support, and promote awareness within communities. By normalizing expressions of grief, respecting cultural diversity, and advocating for inclusive mental health services, societies can create environments where individuals feel supported, validated, and empowered in their journey through sorrow and loss. Continued education, open dialogue, and proactive support are key to cultivating a compassionate response to grief and promoting overall mental well-being.

CHAPTER TEN

Conclusion

Key Insights:

Definition: Post-traumatic growth refers to positive psychological changes that individuals may experience after facing significant adversity or trauma.

Domains of Growth: PTG encompasses several domains, including increased personal strength, appreciation of life, improved relationships, new possibilities, and spiritual or existential growth.

Process of Growth: PTG involves cognitive processing (making sense of the trauma), emotional regulation, behavioral changes, and relational adjustments.

Individual Differences: PTG varies among individuals and is influenced by factors such as personality traits, social support, coping strategies, and the nature of the trauma.

Implications:

Enhanced Resilience: PTG often leads to increased resilience, enabling individuals to cope with future challenges more effectively.

Clinical Practices: Mental health practices are evolving to incorporate interventions that support PTG alongside addressing trauma-related disorders like PTSD.

Narratives and Education: Recognizing PTG shifts the narrative of trauma from solely negative to also acknowledging opportunities for growth and transformation.

Research and Ethics: Ongoing research explores factors contributing to PTG and ethical considerations in supporting trauma survivors' journeys towards growth and recovery.

Takeaways:

Holistic Perspective: PTG offers a holistic perspective on trauma recovery, emphasizing resilience and personal growth alongside healing from trauma-related symptoms.

Hope and Empowerment: Acknowledging PTG provides hope and empowers individuals by highlighting their potential for strength and transformation.

Supportive Environments: Creating supportive environments—through therapy, community support, and education—can facilitate PTG and enhance overall well-being.

Continued Exploration: Continued research and understanding of PTG are essential for developing effective interventions and supporting individuals' journeys of growth after trauma.

Overall, post-traumatic growth underscores the human capacity to find meaning, resilience, and positive change even in the aftermath of profound adversity, offering a profound shift in how we understand and support individuals facing trauma.

Final reflections on the role of sorrow in human life

Sorrow, despite its often painful and challenging nature, plays a profound and complex role in human life, influencing our emotions, relationships, and personal growth in significant ways. Here are some final reflections on the role of sorrow:

1. Depth of Human Experience

Sorrow is a deeply human experience that touches every individual at some point in life. It encompasses feelings of grief, sadness, loss, and anguish, highlighting our capacity for empathy and emotional depth.

2. Catalyst for Growth and Resilience

While sorrow can be overwhelming, it can also serve as a catalyst for personal growth and resilience. Through sorrow, individuals confront their vulnerabilities, reassess priorities, and develop inner strength and coping mechanisms.

3. Reflection and Meaning-Making

Sorrow prompts deep reflection on life's challenges, losses, and uncertainties. It encourages individuals to seek meaning, make sense of difficult experiences, and find a renewed sense of purpose or direction.

4. Connection and Compassion

Experiencing sorrow fosters empathy and compassion towards others who are suffering. It strengthens bonds within families, communities, and society, as individuals come together to provide support and comfort.

5. Spiritual and Existential Inquiry

Sorrow often raises existential questions about life, death, and the nature of suffering.

It can deepen spiritual beliefs, prompt existential exploration, and lead to a deeper understanding of oneself and the world.

6. Transformation and Healing

While sorrow may initially cause pain and disruption, it also holds the potential for profound transformation and healing. It challenges individuals to grow emotionally, psychologically, and spiritually, fostering resilience and adaptation.

7. Navigating Complexity

Navigating sorrow requires patience, self-compassion, and acceptance of one's emotions. It involves embracing the full spectrum of human experience, including both joy and sorrow, as integral parts of life.

8. Honoring Memories and Loss

Sorrow allows individuals to honor memories of loved ones and acknowledge the significance of their absence. It keeps connections alive through remembrance and rituals, contributing to a sense of continuity and legacy.

9. Seeking Support and Community

Seeking support from others—whether through family, friends, support groups, or professional help—is crucial in navigating sorrow. It validates emotions, provides comfort, and offers opportunities for shared healing.

10. Embracing Resilience

Ultimately, sorrow teaches us about resilience—the ability to adapt, grow, and find hope even in the face of adversity. It reminds us of our capacity to endure, heal, and emerge stronger from life's challenges.

In conclusion, while sorrow represents a profound aspect of human existence—one that brings pain and sorrow—it also offers opportunities for reflection, growth, and connection. By embracing sorrow with compassion and resilience, individuals can navigate its complexities, find meaning amidst hardship, and ultimately cultivate a deeper appreciation for the richness of human experience.

Encouragement for readers to embrace and understand their own sorrows

Embracing and understanding our sorrows is a courageous and transformative journey that allows us to navigate life's challenges with greater resilience and compassion. Here's some encouragement for embracing and understanding your own sorrows:

Acknowledge Your Emotions

1. Embrace Your Feelings: Allow yourself to acknowledge and experience your emotions fully, whether it's sadness, grief, or heartache. Recognize that these feelings are valid and part of the human experience.

2. Validate Your Experience: Understand that sorrow is a natural response to loss, disappointment, or difficult circumstances. Validate your experience without judgment or criticism.

Seek Meaning and Growth

3. Reflect and Learn: Take time to reflect on the deeper meaning behind your sorrows. What can you learn from these experiences? How have they shaped your beliefs, values, and priorities?

4. Find Purpose: Explore how your sorrows can lead to personal growth and transformation. Use them as opportunities to reassess your goals, strengthen your resilience, and deepen your understanding of yourself and others.

Connect with Support

5. Reach Out: Don't hesitate to seek support from trusted friends, family members, or mental health professionals. Sharing your sorrows with others can provide comfort, validation, and perspective.

6. Join Communities: Consider joining support groups or communities where you can connect with others who have similar

experiences. Sharing stories and support can be empowering and healing.

Practice Self-Compassion

7. Be Kind to Yourself: Practice self-compassion by treating yourself with kindness, understanding, and patience during difficult times. Allow yourself space to heal and grow at your own pace.

8. Engage in Self-Care: Prioritize self-care activities that nurture your physical, emotional, and spiritual well-being. This may include exercise, mindfulness practices, hobbies, or spending time in nature.

Embrace Resilience

9. Cultivate Resilience: Recognize your inner strength and resilience in facing adversity. Trust in your ability to overcome challenges and bounce back from difficult experiences.

10. Foster Hope: Maintain a sense of hope and optimism for the future, knowing that sorrows are temporary and can lead to

profound personal growth and wisdom over time.

Conclusion

Embracing and understanding your sorrows is not about avoiding pain, but rather about embracing your humanity and finding meaning in your experiences. By allowing yourself to feel, reflect, and seek support, you can navigate sorrows with courage and compassion, ultimately transforming them into opportunities for healing, growth, and resilience. Remember, you are not alone in your journey, and there is strength in embracing your sorrows as part of your unique and meaningful life story.

Additional resources for further reading and support

Books:

"The Wild Edge of Sorrow: Rituals of Renewal and the Sacred Work of Grief" by Francis Weller

This book explores the healing power of grief and offers rituals and practices for navigating sorrow as a transformative process.

"Option B: Facing Adversity, Building Resilience, and Finding Joy" by Sheryl Sandberg and Adam Grant

Sheryl Sandberg shares her personal journey of grief and resilience after the sudden death of her husband, offering insights into building resilience and finding joy amidst adversity.

"When Things Fall Apart: Heart Advice for Difficult Times" by Pema Chödrön

Pema Chödrön, a Buddhist nun, provides compassionate guidance and practical teachings on embracing difficult emotions, including sorrow, as opportunities for growth and spiritual awakening.

"The Year of Magical Thinking" by Joan Didion

Joan Didion's memoir explores grief and mourning following the sudden death of her husband, reflecting on the complexities of loss and resilience.

Websites and Online Resources:

The Dougy Center for Grieving Children & Families

Website: dougy.org

Provides resources, articles, and support for individuals and families navigating grief and loss.

Grief.com

Website: grief.com

Offers articles, podcasts, and resources on grief, including insights from grief expert David Kessler.

National Alliance for Grieving Children (NAGC)

Website: childrengrieve.org

Provides resources, support, and information for children, teens, and families grieving the death of a loved one.

Psychology Today - Grief and Loss

Website: psychologytoday.com/us/basics/grief

Offers articles, blogs, and resources on grief, loss, and coping strategies.

Support Groups and Organizations:

Local Hospice Organizations

Many hospice organizations offer grief support groups, counseling services, and workshops for individuals and families coping with loss.

Online Support Groups

Websites such as GriefShare and Online Grief Support provide virtual support groups and forums for individuals grieving the loss of a loved one.

Local Community Centers and Churches

Community centers, religious organizations, and churches often offer grief support groups, bereavement counseling, and memorial services for individuals and families.

Therapy and Counseling Services:

Find a Therapist

Websites like Psychology Today and Therapist Locator can help you find licensed therapists specializing in grief and loss in your area.

Grief Counseling Services

Many mental health clinics, hospitals, and counseling centers offer specialized grief counseling services provided by licensed therapists and counselors.

These resources can provide valuable information, support, and guidance as you navigate the complexities of sorrow and grief. Remember, seeking support and engaging in self-care are essential steps in healing and finding meaning during difficult times.

……***……